W9-BUU-885

SIGNS OF LIFE

Other Books by Scott Hahn

The Lamb's Supper: The Mass as Heaven on Earth

Hail, Holy Queen: The Mother of God in the Word of God

First Comes Love: Finding Your Family in the Church and the Trinity

Lord, Have Mercy: The Healing Power of Confession

Swear to God: The Promise and Power of the Sacraments

Letter and Spirit: From Written Text to Living Word in the Liturgy

Reasons to Believe: How to Understand, Explain, and Defend the Catholic Faith

Ordinary Work, Extraordinary Grace: My Spiritual Journey in Opus Dei

Understanding the Scriptures: A Complete Course on Bible Study

Scripture Matters: Essays on Reading the Bible from the Heart of the Church

Understanding "Our Father": Biblical Reflections on the Lord's Prayer

A Father Who Keeps His Promises: God's Covenant Love in Scripture

Rome Sweet Home: Our Journey to Catholicism (with Kimberly Hahn)

Living the Mysteries: A Guide for Unfinished Christians (with Mike Aquilina)

SIGNS OF LIFE

40 Catholic Customs and Their Biblical Roots

SCOTT HAHN

DOUBLEDAY

New York • London • Toronto • Sydney • Auckland

DD
DOUBLEDAY

Published in the United States by Doubleday Religion, an imprint of the Crown Publishing Group, a division of Random House, Inc., New York.
www.crownpublishing.com

Nihil Obstat: Monsignor Michael F. Hull, STD, Censor Librorum.
Imprimatur: Most Reverend Dennis J. Sullivan, Auxiliary Bishop and Vicar General, Archdiocese of New York

The *Nihil Obstat* and *Imprimatur* are official declarations that a book or pamphlet is free of doctrinal or moral error. No implication is contained therein that those who have granted the *Nihil Obstat* or *Imprimatur* agree with the content, opinions, or statements expressed.

Library of Congress Cataloging-in-Publication Data
Hahn, Scott.
Signs of Life : 40 Catholic Customs and Their Biblical Roots / by Scott Hahn. — 1st ed.
p. cm.
1. Catholic Church—Doctrines. 2. Catholic Church—Customs and practices. I. Title.
BX1754.H16 2009
282—dc22 2009012276

ISBN: 978-0-385-51949-6

PRINTED IN THE UNITED STATES OF AMERICA

9 10

To Veronica Margaret Hahn,

my first grandchild

Contents

Introduction

I *Life Begins*

II *Life Times*

III *A Day in the Life*

IV *Life Lessons*

V *Stages of Life*

VI *Spice of Life*

VII *Abundant Life*

Introduction

Signs of Life

No matter what line of work we're in, no matter the circumstances of our personal life, we all come to days when we face a wall—a wall too sheer to climb, too high to vault, too strong to topple. These walls can arise, for instance, as problems on the job or in relationships. We try everything humanly possible to get over, around, under, or through them. But we reach a point where there's nothing left to try.

I've faced many of those moments, and one I recall vividly. I was a young scholar, with a young family. I was working on my doctoral thesis, the crowning work of my studies in theology, and I came upon a problem in the interpretation of a certain verse of the Bible. It was a small passage, but it was a big problem, and the verse itself was a key to my argument. So I had to work out all the interpretive kinks before I could defend my thesis before the interrogators on my doctoral committee. In fact, *unless* I worked out the kinks, I was almost sure to fail.

I read all the available commentaries and found nothing useful—not a single glimmer of light, except the sympathy of scholars who had faced the same wall before I did. I dithered and puttered and pondered and paced—for months—but I couldn't find a way forward. This was a real problem, as I had already invested several years in my research. If I abandoned the project now, I faced a long, hard, and humiliating trek back to the beginning of the thesis-approval process.

Then the wall got even higher.

My adviser, a Jesuit priest, called to inform me that he had been transferred to Rome, Italy, to the Gregorian University. I had to complete my dissertation immediately, he said, or search out a new adviser, who might or might not find my thesis plausible.

I stopped sleeping and intensified my efforts, poring over tomes and making late-night calls to scholars I had never met.

Nothing. The wall loomed higher now than ever. On the far side of the wall stretched a professorial career . . . the possibility of tenure . . . open doors for honors, jobs, and publications. On this side, at least as I saw it: professional ruin.

I put myself through several weeks of this when something truly remarkable happened. My adviser called again. He just wanted to make sure I was prepared for *anything* that could happen when I showed up to defend my thesis. And so he went through a list of potential difficulties and obstacles I had not considered before, but that I should expect to encounter on the big day.

I recognized defeat. But I could not admit it. I was too proud. Yet I recognized that, too, as a problem. On top of all that, I was sleep deprived and overcaffeinated, which made my mind a tangle of moral and academic problems of biblical proportions.

There was nothing left for me to do. So I had to do *something.*

Cross Purposes

I had been Roman Catholic only a short while by the time of this crisis—a little less than a decade—but my memory and imagination were already stuffed full of incidents from the lives of the saints, as any ten-year-old's should be.

Please don't get me wrong. I'm not saying I'm a Francis of Assisi or Ignatius Loyola. Nor am I trying to turn up the melodrama. In the great sweep of history, my thesis mattered little. In my professional life, however, it was make or break. The biographies of the saints, I've learned over the years, are made to serve as models for precisely this sort of crisis.

The wall was very high. Yet, very late one night, and quite suddenly, I knew of something much higher than that wall, and I knew what I must do. I put on my jacket and set off into the night, not even bothering to comb my hair.

The neighborhood streets were still and dark. The quickest way to the campus where I teach is straight up the street and through the woods, so that's the way I went.

My goal—the thing so much higher than my wall—was always before me on the horizon. Towering above the dorms and library and labs of Franciscan University of Steubenville is a sixty-foot steel cross, illuminated and visible from the interstate highways, and even from across the Ohio River in West Virginia.

I made my way hastily across the silent campus. If anyone had seen me, they would surely have concluded that too much studying had made me crazy (see Acts 26:24). My mind was surely vexed, but probably as sound as it had ever been, as I found myself at the foot of that shining, colossal cross.

There I didn't have to think hard. I knew what the saints of history had done. I needed to do something. I needed to do what they did.

I kissed the cross, and then I lay flat, face down at the foot of the cross, and I cried.

By then I had filled myself up with all the best the world had to offer. I had consulted the most respected research libraries and personally called upon the top rank of scholars. None of that was enough. And I told that to Jesus: my wall was far too high. Yet I knew, no matter what I was going through, his cross was still higher.

For he had at his disposal a lot more than I had. Nevertheless, even *though he was God,* "he did not count equality with God a thing to be grasped, but emptied himself, taking the form of a servant, being born in the likeness of men. And being found in human form he humbled himself and became obedient unto death, even death on a cross" (Phil 2:6–8).

Lying there with my face in the dirt, I gave him everything, in the way I knew from St. Francis and countless others. I told him that if I had to fail, so be it: I would be emptied as he was.

Here's Mud in Your Eye

What happened next?

I'll get to that in a few minutes. First I'd like to stop and consider the beauty of the Catholic life.

Sometimes we find that we've arrived at a wall. Sometimes we find that we've just hit the wall, at high speed—and we've left our crash helmet at home. When that happens, something in our nature cries out to us: *Don't just stand there. Do something!* God created us that way. He created us with bodies built for action, and he set us to work in a world full of things to do.

All through history, he has acknowledged this natural tendency and given us things to do. When the people were thirsty, God instructed Moses to strike a rock so that water would gush forth. Why did he do that? Not because he needed to. He could have dropped canteens from the clouds, or installed a great lake in the midst of the desert, or even had angels serve up pitchers of margaritas. Yet he knew human nature, and he knew our need to *do something*. So he gave Moses something to do.

From the time of Moses to the time of Jesus, nothing about human nature had changed. Jesus could have cured the blind with a simple nod or a word, but he didn't. He made a paste of mud and spit, and then he sent the blind man off to wash in a nearby pond.

Still another time, Jesus made the healing of lepers contingent on their going to show themselves to the Temple priests. "And as they went they were cleansed" (Lk 17:14).

The Catholic life—the great Christian tradition—is a tremendous inheritance from two millennia of saints in many lands and circumstances. Being Catholic means never having to say we have nothing left to do. Our prayer is enriched by sacred images and incense, votive candles and rosary beads, waters and oils, gestures and postures, blessings and medals, customs and ceremonies.

Because I was learning to live a Catholic life, I was able to say that even alone at three o'clock in the morning in my study, even in the midst of a professional crisis—even when there was nothing more to do—I could do something.

I could leave immediately and make a pilgrimage.
I could prostrate myself in prayer.
I could venerate the holy cross.
I could invoke the Scriptures.

In fact, I could do all these things, and no one was awake to stop me. So I did.

Putting Things in Order

The Catholic life is full of such things. Yet we don't always understand why they're in our tradition. Even devout Catholics can treat these many and diverse customs as if they're disconnected and random acts—superstitions that have somehow gained the Church's approval.

For this reason, you'll sometimes hear Catholic intellectuals sneer at popular piety. That's the last thing I want to do, first of all because Jesus had greater praise for simple believers and children than he had for the intellectuals of his day, and I assume the same rules of human nature still apply. Second of all, because I know that Catholic popular devotions are indeed well-grounded in Scripture—as I hope to show in the course of this book—and that they were practiced by the leading lights of the Catholic intellectual tradition. Finally, because I know many people who are holier than I am but have had no opportunities for theological education. In fact, many canonized saints had no formal education whatsoever. So intellectuals would do well to pray their beads along with the pious sodalities in the parish. It beats sneering any day of the week. Louis Pasteur was one of the intellectual giants of the modern age; yet he prayed his Rosary like a child.

What's more, it's a mistake to treat *intelligence* and *piety* as if they're mutually exclusive terms. The best thing we can do is to offer our devotions with understanding. Jesus instructed us not to pray like theologians who are hypocrites (Mt 6:5); but neither does he want us to pray like pagans who don't have a clue what they're doing (Mt 6:7). A saint of the twentieth century, St. Josemaría Escrivá, put the matter very well. He urged Catholics to have both the wisdom of theologians and the piety of children.

As Catholics, we are free to cultivate a rich life of piety, drawing from the treasures of many lands and many ages. "But," as St. Paul said, "all things should be done decently and in order" (1 Cor 14:40).

This book, then, is a celebration of all things Catholic, and the biblical doctrine that makes them Catholic. But it's more than that. It's a handbook, a how-to, a good-natured defense, and a gentle nudge for all of us to do better, no matter where we are in our spiritual development.

One of my goals in writing this book is to show how Catholic customs and devotions fit into the larger scheme of Christian faith. Our first order of business is to develop a new way of seeing, a new way of growing in wisdom and knowledge. That way is traditionally called *mystagogy*.

Reading the Signs

The English word *mystagogy* comes from the Greek *mystagogia*, which means "guidance in the mysteries." In the mystagogical instruction of the early Church, a clergyman (usually the local bishop) would take the time to explain the small details of the liturgy and how they corresponded symbolically to the events that played out in the Bible. This method reaches back to the New Testament itself, where St. Paul and St. Peter spoke of baptism and Eucharist as the fulfillment of Old Testament foreshadowings (see, for example, 1 Cor 10:2–17; 1 Pet 3:18–21).

Mystagogy enables new believers to see beyond the signs to the things signified—to see beyond the here and now and glimpse the divine mysteries that will one day be fully visible to us in heaven (1 Jn 3:2) but even now are truly present in the Church.

We may hear the story of the great flood and, through instruction, prayer, and meditation, discern the saving waters of baptism. But further, we may see beyond the sign of baptism and discern the work of the Holy Spirit, because the third person of the Blessed Trinity *is* the ultimate reality signified and conveyed by the waters of baptism.

For even Jesus' miracles—great as they were—served primarily as "signs." That is the word St. John used to describe them (see, for example, Jn 2:11 and 4:54). They were real events, and they were momentous, but still they pointed beyond themselves, to a divine and transcendent reality. Consider Jesus' healing of the paralyzed man (Mk 2:3–12). Our Lord made it clear that curing paralysis was a lesser deed than the forgiveness of sins. The physical healing was simply an outward sign of the greater healing, the inner, spiritual healing. The physical cure, after all, was a temporary reprieve; eventually the man's life would run its natural course, and he would suffer and die. The spiritual healing, however, could last even beyond death; it made for a new creation, an act possible by no one but God (Mk 2:7).

Jesus has given us the privilege of sharing in the life and saving actions of God. At the Last Supper, he spoke of his miraculous signs and then promised his apostles: "Truly, truly, I say to you, he who believes in me will also do the works that I do; and greater works than these will he do" (Jn 14:12). Though the apostles did perform miracles during their ministry, they did nothing that exceeded Jesus' miracles in grandeur. So what could he have meant?

He meant the sacraments.

The early Christians believed in the sacraments. They believed that the sacraments not only spoke *about* Jesus' divine power—but rather they *spoke Jesus' divine power.* All words signify things. Yet, in the Gospels, Jesus' word brought about the realities it signified. He spoke and demons were cast out, people were cured of their illnesses, raging winds and waters were stilled, the dead were raised. That same divine Word still has the power to transform the things of creation and the moments of our lives. It does so through the ministry of the Church, which uses the stuff of the earth—bread and wine, gestures and postures, oil and water—to bring holiness into our lives. This happens in the sacraments, which the ancient Church referred to as "mysteries." In the fifth century, Pope St. Leo the Great said: "What was visible in our Savior has passed over into his mysteries." Thus, mystagogy is rooted in God's grace: his power to change us.

That power is hidden to our natural senses. Mystagogy, on the other hand, is the Church's traditional way of revealing it to our mind and spirit. It is the saints' way of revealing the divine love that abides behind the symbols, the divine life that lives beyond the signs. In the holy things of our tradition, material objects show us immaterial realities—temporal events disclose eternal mysteries.

Mystagogy means leading believers into a real communion, a real sharing, in the saving mysteries celebrated in the symbols and rituals of the Church's worship. Pope Benedict XVI once said: "The mature fruit of mystagogy is an awareness that one's life is being progressively transformed by the holy mysteries being celebrated . . . mak[ing] him a 'new creation.' "

Living the Mysteries

For the early Christians, the mystery of Christ was not limited to the sacramental rituals. It touched also upon morals and everyday life. It was God's "plan for the fullness of time," after all, "to unite all things in him, things in heaven and things on earth" (Eph 1:10). In Christ "all things were created, in heaven and on earth, visible and invisible . . . all things were created through him and for him . . . and in him all things hold together" (Col 1:16–17).

Thus, in Christ, all the things of the earth become signposts pointing us to God. The things of the earth are not to be despised, but rather sanctified, raised up, made holy by holy use. In the Mass we offer God the "work of human hands." In our work we do the same. We do no less in our devotion. We pray, according to our customs, as the early Christians did, with sacraments as well as *sacramentals.*

What is a sacramental?

It is any object set apart and blessed by the Church to lead us to good thoughts and increase our devotion. A sacramental is *like* a sacrament in that it is a means of grace and an outward sign of an invisible mystery of faith. It is also *unlike* a sacrament in many ways. Sacraments were instituted by Christ, while sacramentals are established by the Church. Sacraments convey grace *directly* in our souls, while sacramentals do so *indirectly,* by leading us to devotion and providing us an occasion when we may respond to God's grace.

This idea is as old as the Church. In the fourth century St. Gregory of Nyssa preached a splendid homily about this *sacramental principle.* He began by praising God for the power he gave to ordinary things: water in baptism, bread and wine in the Mass, oil in anointing, the press of the bishop's hands in ordination. "There are many things that appear to be contemptible," he said, "but accomplish mighty works." Drawing from the Old Testament, he noted the common items that God had invested with miraculous power: Moses' wooden staff, Elijah's mantle of rough cloth, and the bones of the dead Elisha.

St. Gregory saw that such a dispensation of power had not only continued in his own day, but increased many times over. So it continues into our times, too, offering us manifold graces. In fact, those three examples he gave are the remote ancestors of practices that continue into our own day, practices we'll examine in this book: the veneration of the cross, the wearing of the brown scapular, and the honor we give to the relics of the saints.

Distinct Possibilities

For Catholics, sacraments and sacramentals are unmistakable signs of life. Both are part of this book, as both should be part of our everyday living and loving.

Jesus' own devotional life was very rich. He took part in pilgrimages and festivals. He prayed spontaneously and formally. He prayed kneeling and standing and prostrate. He worshipped alone, with congregations, and with friends. He recited the Scriptures. He went on silent retreats, away from the bustle and distractions of the world.

It is our privilege to imitate him in that beautiful variety, and our tradition gives us many ways of doing so. It's true that not all prayers and devotions are created equal. As we take up the customs of our Catholic faith, it's important that we distinguish between those that are essential and those that we may choose or reject with Christian freedom. We have a strict obligation to be baptized and go to Mass on Sundays and holy days of obligation (see Jn 3:5 and 6:53). We are not obliged, however, to say the Rosary, use holy water, or pray novenas. Nevertheless, sometimes it's the nonessentials that transform a house into a true home. Yes, we need the bricks and mortar to build up a functional shelter; but life is a whole lot richer when we can also smell the aroma of dinner cooking in the kitchen and hear the babbling of small children in the living room. These time-tested devotions really do help to make our faith a *life* and our Church a *home.*

Still, I know that some people will dismiss all habits of piety, objecting that they're just rote and routine habits. They are indeed habits, and we can indeed make them rote and routine. But those qualities, by themselves, are not bad. Rote and routine are quite good, in fact, when we apply them to lawn care, car care, musical performance, or personal hygiene. I maintain, with Catholic tradition, that routines of prayer, when offered from the heart, can be very good for the soul. They are like beautiful music or gardens tended with care—rote habits rooted in love.

Others will object that these actions are medieval superstitions or attempts to manipulate God. But that's simply not so. By offering our prayers, we're not getting God to do our bidding; we're allowing God to have his way. These ways of prayer are divine mercies, a language God fosters so we will speak with him regularly and often, whether we feel like it or not. Our devotions are not primarily what we do for God—he does not need our praise or our incense—but rather what he does for us. These modes of communication conform remarkably well to the human mind and body, which God himself created for his glory.

How the Book Works

In this book, we'll examine forty different traditional practices of the Church. Why did I choose forty? The number, of course, has a rich pedigree. The Bible speaks of the forty days when flood waters purified the earth . . . of the forty years that Israel spent sojourning in the desert . . . of the forty days Elijah spent on his journey . . . of the forty days the people of Nineveh repented because of the preaching of the prophet Jonah . . . of the forty days that Jesus fasted in the wilderness . . . and of the forty days he remained with the disciples, between his resurrection and ascension. The Church, early on, noted this pattern as it established the forty-day season of Lent.

So forty seemed to me to be a good number. I hope these meditations, like those biblical forties, will be for you and me a time of purification, transformation, and renewal. I hope these pages can be our journey together, toward a richer and fuller understanding of the Catholic life.

But there's nothing canonical about the forty customs I chose. My selection is not quite random, but not quite inevitable either. It's mine. And I hope that, as you grow in devotion, you'll make a list that's your own.

In the same way, the meditations are not definitions. They're my reflections, borrowed from this saint and that pope and combined in a way that's mine (and not definitive). I hope you'll reflect on each sign in a way that's grounded in the tradition, but truly your own.

The sequence of chapters is mine as well. It's not exactly continuous, but I intended it to be cumulative in its effect. Some chapters do build upon information in the chapters that precede them. Like life, the book moves forward, in a meandering way, from birth to death. But you should feel free to jump around, as your interests or needs direct you. You're free to read at the pace you wish, though the book was written to be read slowly and contemplated.

In each chapter we'll look at the deep biblical and historical roots of a particular Catholic custom. We'll find answers to common objections raised by non-Catholics, and we'll try to clear up some common misconceptions. Each chapter concludes with a "Ponder in Your Heart" section. The title refers to Luke's description of the Blessed Virgin: "Mary kept all these things, pondering them in her heart" (Lk 2:19). I'm hoping that you and I can imitate her as we ponder the words of Christian history's great teachers, thinkers, and saints. I chose these "Ponder" passages from the tradition. I've included passages from most, if not all, of the centuries from Jesus' to our own. Taken all together, they make an important point: that these doctrines and devotions are not my inventions, that they have been confirmed by tradition, and that they work. They've helped other Catholics, many Catholics, down through the centuries, mark their way to heaven. I chose passages from a variety of authors. I chose the passages I have found most helpful.

The idea here is to heighten our awareness of our faith, to make our devotions as *everyday* as possible. We want to form good *habits* of prayer—or, to use the more intimidating modern term: *disciplines* of prayer. The sacramental principle works so well because it presupposes the fundamental reality of human nature: we are composed of body and soul, a material body and a spiritual soul. What we do to one component profoundly affects the other. What we do with our body, our senses, provides the foundation for our spiritual growth. Grace builds on nature.

There are many good, natural reasons to take up the traditional methods of prayer. Physiologists recognize that they relax our bodies, reduce our stress levels, and unfurrow our brows. They also burn durable neural pathways. Anyone who has spent time by the deathbeds of faithful Catholics can testify, as I can: there are certain devotions that seem fairly consistently to remain to the very end of consciousness, even when much else has vanished from memory. I have a dear friend whose mother survived a stroke with little left but the ability to recite the Rosary—a habit ingrained over a long lifetime. It proved to be her path to recovery. I could tell hundreds of stories like this one.

So it makes no sense to defer the disciplines of prayer till we're older. First, we may not have the luxury of getting older. But even if we do, we may not have the health, memory, or freedom necessary to establish new habits.

It may sound cliché, but we don't know what lies ahead for us. We do know that we'll suffer, you and I, because that's part of life, even life in Christ. But God has provided for those times. He and his Church have given us a storehouse of tradition—methods and counsel that have proven reliable over the course of millennia, through the lives of countless ordinary Christians, through economic depression and natural disasters, through persecution and war. Now that's what I call research and development!

In every trial, God will "provide the way of escape, that you may be able to endure it" (1 Cor 10:13). Even amid the most extraordinary circumstances, we can escape to God, we can endure, and we can prevail, using the most ordinary means of prayer. It is a very good thing if all we need to do is touch a bead or feel the wool of a scapular in order to turn our thoughts to God, because we may come to moments when that's all we *can* do.

I pray you'll pray these prayers, as well as you can, and ask the Holy Spirit and your guardian angel to make up for whatever you lack.

As you pray, please remember to pray for this author—who promises to pray for his readers!

Back to the Cross

Oh, yes, I promised to finish my story about my dissertation.

I returned home saying the Rosary, by way of my neighborhood's darkened streets, but I felt as if it was broad daylight. Once back in my office, I returned to the biblical text—which I had read hundreds and possibly thousands of times—and read it as if for the first time. In fact, I encountered it as if I were the first person reading it. In the original Greek I saw connections that had not made it cleanly into the English and Latin translations.

To cut to the chase: I found a solution that, till then, had appeared nowhere else in the commentaries. I finished my dissertation and defended it successfully. I wrote up my findings and published them in a major scholarly journal.

Twelve years after that fateful, faithful night, I was attending a professional conference, the annual meeting of the Society of Biblical Literature, when a scholar I respect took me aside and asked: "How does it feel to have nailed it?"

I had no idea what he was talking about.

"How does it feel," he asked, "to have found the interpretation that had been lost to the ages?"

Then I knew what he meant, and my eyes welled up.

I told him the story about a night long ago, a wall too high for me to scale. I told him of my journey to the cross. I wanted him to know the way, in case he, too, should find himself at a wall.

I want the same for you, and that's the reason for the rest of this book.

I

Life Begins

1.

Holy Water

We begin in water.

That's how the book of Genesis poetically depicts the creation of the universe: "darkness was upon the face of the deep; and the Spirit of God was moving over the face of the waters . . . And God said, 'Let there be a firmament in the midst of the waters, and let it separate the waters from the waters' " (Gen 1:2, 6).

As it was in the cosmic, so it is in our personal beginnings: we assume our human form in the amniotic sac, "bag of waters," in the womb. In the order of nature, birth begins when a mother's "water breaks."

So with water we begin our visits to church. We dip a hand into a holy-water font, and we bless ourselves.

There has been a watermark on Christian prayer since the earliest days of the Church. At the end of the second century, a North African theologian named Tertullian mentions the custom of symbolically cleansing one's hands before lifting them in prayer. It was a Jewish custom that predated the coming of Our Lord, and it may be what St. Paul was referring to when he wrote to Timothy: "I desire then that in every place the men should pray, lifting holy hands" or "pure hands" (I Tim 2:8). The historian Eusebius, writing around A.D. 320, describes a church in Tyre that had flowing fountains at its entrance, where the faithful might purify their hands.

We use water to mark our beginnings because God does. We find ample evidence of this in both nature and Scripture. When the world was lost to sin and needed cleansing and rebirth, God sent a great flood, and from that flood the family of Noah found new life. When Israel emerged from slavery as a unified nation, it first had to pass through the waters of the Red Sea. When the chosen people established their places of worship—first the tabernacle and then the Temple—they constructed them with bronze basins for washing upon entry.

St. Thomas Aquinas taught that water has been a natural sacrament since the dawn of creation. In the age of nature—from Adam through the patriarchs—water refreshed and cleansed humankind. In the age of Law—the time of Moses—water provided a spiritual rebirth for Israel as the nation began its journey to the promised land. With Jesus, however, came the age of grace; and from that time onward water received the divine power of the Word made flesh. Though babies had always been born through "water," now grown men and women could be "born of water and the Holy Spirit" (Jn 3:5). The Church Fathers taught that Jesus, by descending into the waters of the River Jordan, had sanctified the waters of the world. He made them living and life-giving (see Jn 4:10–14). He made them a source of *supernatural* regeneration, refreshment, and cleansing.

While we are on earth, we know spiritual things by means of

sensible signs. It is only in glory that we will see divine things as they are, without their sacramental veils. According to St. Thomas, water ultimately "signifies the grace of the Holy Spirit . . . For the Holy Spirit is the unfailing fountain from whom all gifts of grace flow." The book of Revelation confirms this, as it presents the Spirit's grace as a "river of the water of life, bright as crystal, flowing from the throne of God and of the Lamb" (Rev 22:1).

Through history and through the cosmos, God has spoken with a voice that is "like the sound of many waters" (Rev 1:15). All the many sacred meanings of water we take for our own and claim as our inheritance—whenever we bless ourselves with holy water.

"Beloved, we are God's children now," born of water and the Spirit. "And everyone who thus hopes in him purifies himself as he is pure" (1 Jn 3:2-3).

This simple action, which even the smallest children love to do, is a reminder and a renewal of our baptism. It is a refreshment, too, providing relief from the oppression of evil. St. Teresa of Avila wrote that "there is nothing the devils flee from more—without returning—than holy water."

Holy water is ordinary water that has been blessed for devotional use by a priest. We bless ourselves with holy water at church. Most churches also provide a dispenser so that parishioners can draw water to take home with them. Some Catholic families keep a little holy-water font at the entryway to every bedroom. I keep a bottle of the stuff in my office at all times.

We need do no more with it than splash a few drops on ourselves. It is customary to pronounce a blessing in the name of the Holy Trinity, too, and trace the outline of a cross with our right hand.

That's enough for now. We'll save the rest for the next chapter.

Ponder in Your Heart

King and Lord of all things and maker of the world: you gave salvation freely to all created nature by the descent of your only-begotten Jesus Christ. You redeemed all that you created by the coming of your ineffable Word. See now from heaven, and look upon these waters, and fill them with the Holy Spirit. Let your ineffable Word come to be in them and tranform their energy and cause them to be generative, as being filled with your grace . . . As your only-begotten Word coming down upon the waters of the Jordan rendered them holy, so now may he descend on these and make them holy and spiritual.

—Blessing of Water, from the sacramentary of St. Serapion of Egypt, fourth century

2.

The Sign of the Cross

What water is to elements, the Sign of the Cross is to gestures. Cardinal Joseph Ratzinger (the future Pope Benedict XVI) once wrote: "The most basic Christian gesture in prayer is and always will be the Sign of the Cross."

This is the most common prayer of Christians, and it has been since the founding of the Church. St. Paul speaks of the cross in almost all his New Testament letters: "But far be it from me to glory except in the cross of our Lord Jesus Christ, by which the world has been crucified to me, and I to the world" (Gal 6:14).

We could fill a book with the early Christians' testimonies to this practice. It was their favorite devotion as it required no special knowledge or skill. You didn't have to be literate to make the Sign of the Cross, or rich enough to own a book of instructions. All you needed was one working finger. Martyrs made the Sign as they were taken to their death. Even Julian, the notoriously ex-Christian emperor, fell back to tracing the Sign whenever he felt oppressed by demons.

It is mentioned everywhere because it was practiced everywhere. At the end of the second century, Tertullian proclaimed: "In all our travels and movements, in all our coming in and going out, in putting on our shoes, at the bath, at the table, in lighting our candles, in lying down, in sitting down, whatever task occupies us, we mark our forehead with the sign of the cross." Tertullian praised his wife for her virtues, her beauty, and her wardrobe, but preeminently because she made the Sign of the Cross over her body and over her bed before retiring for the night.

The earliest accounts suggest that Christians traced the cross with their thumb upon their forehead. They also traced it on objects, such as food, and over the sacramental elements: bread, wine, oil, and water.

Over the centuries the faithful have developed many ways of doing it. In the Western churches, we bless ourselves with our open right hand, touching our fingertips to the forehead, then the breastbone, then the left shoulder, and finally the right shoulder. Some interpret the five open fingers as a sign of the Five Wounds of Christ.

In the Mass, just before the Gospel, we use another form as well: a "Small Sign of the Cross," in which we trace with our thumb a cruciform on our forehead and lips, and over our heart. When the priest or deacon does this, we can sometimes hear him say quietly: "The Lord be in my heart and on my lips that I may worthily proclaim his holy Gospel." People who use the Small Sign in private devotions sometimes offer it with the Latin prayer *Per signum crucis de inimicis nostris libera nos Deus noster* ("By the sign of the cross, our God, deliver us from our enemies").

Christians of the Eastern churches have their own way of making the Sign. Their placement of fingers turns the hand into a virtual catechism. They join the thumb, index, and middle finger at the fingertips. The three fingers together represent the Trinity in unity. The remaining two fingers—pinky and ring—are pressed together against the palm, and they together symbolize the hypostatic union: the unity of Jesus' human and divine natures.

Some people, in the East and the West, keep the custom of kissing their fingers at the conclusion of the Sign.

Worldwide and throughout history, there are countless variations on the practice and its interpretation. One of my favorite explanations comes from my patron saint, Francis de Sales:

> We raise the hand first to the forehead, saying, "In the name of the Father," to signify that the Father is the first person of the Most Holy Trinity, of whom the Son is begotten and from whom the Holy Spirit proceeds. Then saying, "And the Son," the hand is lowered to the breast, to express that the Son proceeds from the Father, who sent him down to the womb of the Virgin. Then the hand is moved from the left shoulder or side to the right, while saying, "and of the Holy Spirit," thereby signifying that the Holy Spirit, as the third person of the Holy Trinity, proceeds from the Father and the Son, that he is the love that unites both, and that we, through his grace, partake of the fruits of the passion. Accordingly the Sign of the Cross is a brief declaration of our faith in the three great mysteries: of our faith in the Blessed Trinity, in the passion of Christ, and in the forgiveness of sin, by which we pass from the left side of curse to the right of blessing.

The Trinity and the cross: it's not an accident of piety that these two themes converge in the words and gesture of the Church's most fundamental and most popular prayer.

The cross is an image in time of the Trinity's life in eternity. On the cross, Jesus Christ gave himself entirely. He held nothing back.

Such is the self-giving of the Son for the Father, the Father for the Son. Each makes a complete and loving gift of his life to the other, and that gift, that life, that love, is the Holy Spirit. The sign of that love in the world is the Sign of the Cross.

At the end of his struggle, Jesus gave up his Spirit (Jn 19:30) as he pronounced his work "finished," accomplished, fulfilled. When we make the Sign of the Cross, we correspond to that grace. We receive the love he gives. We take on that Spirit as we take up his cross. We see Jesus give himself in love, and we say "Amen!" We accept that life as our own.

It's no small thing we do when we make the Sign of the Cross. It should take our breath away—but only so that we can be filled up with another wind, another breath: the Spirit of God.

This is the life we received in baptism, when we were marked with the Sign and saved from our sins. The early Christians compared this to the mark on the brow of Cain (Gen 4:15), which protected him from the punishment he deserved. They saw it foreshadowed also in the mark of blood on the doorposts that saved the firstborn sons of the Israelites at the Passover (Ex 12:7). They saw it even more vividly depicted in the oracle of the prophet Ezekiel, who saw that the righteous in Jerusalem would one day be saved because of a "mark upon the foreheads" (Ez 9:4). What was that mark? According to the ancient rabbis, it was *tav,* the last letter of the Hebrew alphabet, which in ancient times was drawn as a cross. In the New Testament, in the book of Revelation, St. John saw the faithful in heaven distinguished by this Sign on their foreheads (Rev 14:1, 22:4).

The custom has passed down through the ages, and indeed it will always be with us. In his groundbreaking work on Sacred Tradition, St. Basil the Great identified it as a hallmark of the apostolic faith. It is honored even in heaven, and even by the greatest of saints. At Lourdes, France, in 1858, when the Virgin Mary first appeared to little Bernadette Soubirous, before she uttered a single word, she made the Sign of the Cross.

This simplest gesture is the richest of creeds. It encompasses the infinite. It proclaims the Trinity, the incarnation, and our redemption. It is, in the words of Cardinal Ratzinger, a "summing up and re-acceptance of our baptism." As Pope Benedict XVI, he added: "Making the Sign of the Cross . . . means saying a visible and public 'yes' to the One who died and rose for us, to God who in the humility and weakness of his love is the Almighty, stronger than all the power and intelligence of the world."

Ponder in Your Heart

When we cross ourselves, let it be with a real Sign of the Cross. Instead of a small cramped gesture that gives no notion of its meaning, let us make a large unhurried sign, from forehead to breast, from shoulder to shoulder, consciously feeling how it includes the whole of us, our thoughts, our attitudes, our body and soul, every part of us at once, how it consecrates and sanctifies us . . .

Think of these things when you make the Sign of the Cross. It is the holiest of all signs . . . Let it take in your whole being—body, soul, mind, will, thoughts, feelings, your doing and not-doing—and by signing it with the cross strengthen and consecrate the whole in the strength of Christ, in the name of the triune God.

—Romano Guardini, twentieth century

3.

Baptism

You've probably seen greeting cards that claim "Life begins at forty" or thirty or fifty.

Don't believe them. Life begins at baptism. Baptism is the quintessential "sign of life." Jesus himself spoke of baptism in terms of strict obligation: "unless one is born of water and the Spirit, he cannot enter the kingdom of God" (Jn 3:5). Baptism was the substance of his final earthly command: "Go therefore and make disciples of all nations, baptizing them in the name of the Father and of the Son and of the Holy Spirit" (Mt 28:19). When new believers asked St. Peter, the first pope, what they should do, he infallibly declared: "Repent, and be baptized every one of you" (Acts 2:38).

Just as our natural living cannot proceed without a birth, so our supernatural life cannot proceed without our baptism.

Before our baptism, we may have a beating heart and a lively mind. We may even have an important job and many friends—so that no one would ever dare to tell us to "get a life." Yet, until we're baptized, we don't have the kind of life Jesus talked about when he said: "I am the way, and the truth, and the life; no one comes to the Father, but by me" (Jn 14:6).

His statement is curious, because people can indeed go to God without going by way of Jesus. Even pagans can. St. Paul said so in his Letter to the Romans: "what can be known about God is plain to them, because God has shown it to them" (1:19–20). But here's the difference: they cannot know him as *Father.* And that is the essence of Christianity.

It's easy for us to take God's fatherhood for granted. It has become a rather bland cliché: God is our Father, and we're all brothers and sisters, so let's all get along. We forget that this assertion was once enough to get a man killed: "This was why the Jews sought all the more to kill [Jesus], because he . . . called God his Father" (Jn 5:18). Even today, Muslims consider it blasphemy to attribute fatherhood to God.

Children, whether natural or adopted, must share the same nature as their parents. I might feel an extreme fondness for my pets, but I cannot make them my children, because they do not possess human nature.

Thus, when a person calls God "Father," he is—as Jesus' contemporaries rightly observed—"making himself equal with God" (Jn 5:18), because a father and child must share the same nature.

God's fatherhood is the truth at the heart of Jesus' gospel of salvation. When we are born anew in baptism, we are born not of human parentage, but heavenly: "See what love the Father has given us, that we should be called children of God; and so we are . . . we are God's children now; it does not yet appear what we shall be, but we know that when he appears we shall be like him" (1 Jn 3:1–2).

What can all this mean?

Theologians since ancient times have described our salvation as a "marvelous exchange." In Jesus, God became what we are so that we might become what he is. The Son of God became the Son of Man so that the children of men might become children of God. Through baptism we become "partakers of the divine nature" (2 Pt 1:4). We are baptized *into* Christ, so that we can live *in* him. The early Christians daringly called this process our *divinization* or *deification.* It is, like natural birth, a pure gift, nothing we could ever accomplish or earn for ourselves. We become by grace what God is by nature. That is why God became a man, and that is why he gave us baptism.

Such was God's intention from the beginning of time. The apostles found the waters of baptism abundantly foretold in the Old Testament (see chapter 1). St. Paul, however, saw baptism also as a fulfillment of the ancient Hebrews' practice of circumcising all newborn males: "you were circumcised with a circumcision made without hands, by putting off the body of flesh in the circumcision of Christ; and you were buried with him in baptism" (Col 2:11–12). The circumcision of infants, then, prefigured the baptism of those who would be "newborn" in Christ. The old rite marked a child's "birth" as a son of Abraham; the new rite marks the still greater birth of a child of God.

To be precise: with circumcision, a boy entered into God's *covenant* with the family of Abraham. A covenant is a legal action based upon an oath; its purpose is to create a family bond between formerly unrelated persons. Marriage is a covenant. Adoption is a covenant. God made a covenant with Abraham, so that Abraham's descendants through Isaac would be God's family on earth.

Circumcision was the preeminent sign of the Old Covenant (see Acts 7:8). God welcomed newborns into Israel by means of ritual circumcision—though adult males, too, would undergo the painful rite if they chose to convert to Judaism.

From the beginning the Church, in turn, received infants and adults—and all ages in between—into the family of God by means of baptism, the "circumcision made without hands."

Circumcision was painful. It was costly. It was a down payment in blood that served as a pledge of one's entire life. Yet membership in God's family was well worth the price.

With baptism the rewards are even greater, but the cost is greater, too. St. Ambrose of Milan, writing in the fourth century, put it this way. A man who underwent circumcision endured pain in one part of the body, for a brief time. Yet baptism, he said, is "the sacrament of the cross." Whether an infant or an adult, the Christian who has been "baptized into Christ Jesus" has been "baptized into his death" (Rom 6:3). That death means a new life for us, a "new creation" (2 Cor 5:17; Gal 6:15).

Salvation has not exempted us from suffering. Christ is our "pioneer," precisely because he has suffered (Heb 2:10 and 12:2). A pioneer is not the last to enter a new territory, but the first. He has gone before us, to serve as a model for imitation, and to empower us to follow after him. We live the life of children of God when we live the life of Christ, when we live as he lived, when we suffer as he suffered. By the power of our baptism, we can live his life for all eternity in heaven. For us as for him, it starts here and now. By baptism, we are "conformed to the image of [God's] Son" (Rom 8:29). We are, here and now, "being changed into his likeness from one degree of glory to another" (2 Cor 3:18). This happens not *in spite of* our suffering, but *through* our suffering—which, because of that "marvelous exchange," works in us with divine power, redemptive power.

We must not allow ourselves to be lulled by the clichés about God's fatherhood. The doctrine of baptism is so rich, so radical, and so revolutionary that it was baffling to Nicodemus—who was perhaps the most learned and clever of Jesus' friends (see Jn 3:1–15). Jesus told Nicodemus, in so many words, that he would need the grace of baptism in order to understand the new birth of baptism. The early Church followed the Lord in imparting the doctrine of baptism to adults only *after* they had been baptized. Only then were they capable of approaching the mysteries—and living the mysteries, because baptism had (and has) profound implications for Christian moral life.

For we the baptized are living "in Christ" (see Rom 8:1), and Christ is living in us (Gal 2:20). We are sons and daughters in the eternal Son of God. Though Christ had the "form of God" (Phil 2:6), he poured himself out to take on a human "form" (2:7)—again, so that we might be in him and he in us. "So you also must consider yourselves dead to sin and alive to God in Christ Jesus. Let not sin therefore reign in your mortal bodies, to make you obey their passions. Do not yield your members to sin as instruments of wickedness, but yield yourselves to God as men who have been brought from death to life, and your members to God as instruments of righteousness. For sin will have no dominion over you, since you are not under law but under grace" (Rom 6:11–14).

Baptism is not merely a ceremony, not merely a rite of passage. It is our entry into a New Covenant bond, a new family, a new life, a new birth, a new creation. "We are Christians because of a covenant," said the theologian Romano Guardini. Yet he also lamented that "it is strange how completely the idea of the covenant has vanished from the Christian consciousness. We do mention it, but it seems to have lost its meaning for us." We should take every care to understand our baptism and never underestimate it—and not only our own baptism, but those of our friends and especially our children and godchildren (what a great and sweet responsibility that is). Do you know your baptismal day as well as you know your birthday? Do you mark it in some special way?

Ponder in Your Heart

In considering . . . the gift which comes from baptism, the apostle Peter breaks out into song: "Blessed be the God and Father of our Lord Jesus Christ! By his great mercy we have been born anew to a living hope through the resurrection of Jesus Christ from the dead, and to an inheritance which is imperishable, undefiled and unfading" (I Pt I:3–4). And he calls Christians those who have been "born anew, not of perishable seed but of imperishable, through the living and abiding word of God" (I Pt I:23).

With baptism we become children of God in his only-begotten Son, Jesus Christ. Rising from the waters of the baptismal font, every Christian hears again the voice that was once heard on the banks of the Jordan River: "You are my beloved Son; with you I am well pleased" (Lk 3:22). From this comes the understanding that one has been brought into association with the beloved Son, becoming a child of adoption (cf. Gal 4:4–7) and a brother or sister of Christ. In this way the eternal plan of the Father for each person is realized in history. . .

St. Maximus, Bishop of Turin, in addressing those who had received the holy anointing of baptism, repeats the same sentiments: "Ponder the honor that has made you sharers in this mystery!" All the baptized are invited to hear once again the words of St. Augustine: "Let us rejoice and give thanks: we have not only become Christians, but Christ himself . . . Stand in awe and rejoice: We have become Christ."

—Pope John Paul II, twentieth century

4.

The Mass

Long before the New Testament books were written—before any churches were built, before the first disciple died as a martyr for the faith—the Mass was the center of life for the Church.

St. Luke sums it up in the Acts of the Apostles: "And they devoted themselves to the apostles' teaching and fellowship, to the breaking of bread and the prayers" (Acts 2:42). Luke manages to get so much detail into that single sentence. The first Christians were eucharistic by nature: they gathered for "the breaking of the bread and the prayers." They were formed by the Word of God, the "apostles' teaching." When they met as a Church, their worship culminated in "fellowship"—the Greek word is *koinonia,* communion.

The Mass was the center of life for the disciples of Jesus, and so it has ever been. Even today, the Mass is where we experience the apostolic teaching and communion, the breaking of the bread and the prayers.

St. Luke focuses primarily on the externals, which are mighty by themselves, but the Mass is still so much more.

The first Christians were Jews, living in a Jewish culture, steeped in Jewish forms of worship. They saw the Eucharist as the fulfillment of all the rites of the Old Covenant. Jesus' sacrifice had rendered Israel's ceremonial laws obsolete, but it had not dispensed entirely with ritual worship. Jesus himself established rites for the New Covenant: baptism (Mt 28:19), for example, and sacramental absolution (Jn 20:22–23). He reserved the greatest solemnity, however, for the Eucharist (Lk 22:20).

The liturgy of the new covenant had been foreshadowed in the rituals of the old. The Gospels make an explicit connection between the Mass and the Passover meal (Lk 22:15). The Epistle to the Hebrews sees the Mass in light of the Temple's animal sacrifices (Heb 13:10). Many modern scholars have noted parallels between the Mass and the most commonly offered sacrifice of Jesus' day: the thank-offering (in Hebrew, *todah*). The todah was a sacrificial meal of bread and wine, shared with his friends, given in thanksgiving for God's deliverance. The Talmud records the ancient rabbis' teaching that, when the Messiah has come, "all sacrifices will cease except the todah sacrifice. This will never cease in all eternity." When the Jews translated their Scriptures into Greek, they rendered the word *todah* as *eucharistia,* the word from which we get "Eucharist."

All of Israel's traditions of worship were like mighty rivers that flowed into the infinite ocean of adoration that Jesus established for the Church. There they did not vanish, but found completion.

Many years before he became pope, Cardinal Joseph Ratzinger wrote of yet another notion from ancient Jewish ritual. *Chaburah* was the word used to describe the fellowship shared by members of God's covenant family. They shared *chaburah* with one another. They ate *chaburah* meals together. On the eve of a Sabbath or holy day, a rabbi would customarily share such a supper with his disciples. When Jews translated the word into Greek, they rendered it as *koinonia*, communion. The divine covenant brought about powerful fellowship among the people of God.

But the Jews stopped short of describing any *chaburah* between God and human beings. They believed such communion to be impossible. The very idea would be an affront to God's transcendence. God, after all, is infinite, perfect, and all-good. We are finite, imperfect, and sinful. How could two parties so vastly different enjoy communion with one another, when one party is so clearly unworthy?

God himself disregarded the threat of defilement; and by means of the new covenant, he himself established communion with his people: all of us in the Church, and each of us in the Church. This may be why the language of "covenant," which is everywhere in the Old Testament, appears rarely in the New Testament; it is replaced by the language of communion. The Mass, said Jesus, "is the new covenant in my blood" (1 Cor 11:25); but now, in this *New* Covenant, he has raised the stakes. He has given the Mass as "a communion [*koinonia*] in the blood of Christ" (1 Cor 10:16).

The apostles made clear that Jesus' salvation had shattered not only the boundaries between Israel and the nations, but also between God and the world. Yes, fellowship was now possible among all peoples, both Jews and Gentiles. God's family would at last be universal.

Now, too, God himself would share communion with his people. Our life in Christ is our sharing, our participation, our communion in God's life. It is, at last, *chaburah* between God and mankind.

Ancient Israel had always considered its earthly liturgy to be a divinely inspired imitation of heavenly worship. What the priests did in the Temple was an earthly imitation of what the angels did in heaven. Yet it was still only an imitation, only a *shadow.*

By assuming human flesh, the eternal Son of God brought heaven to earth. No longer must the people of God worship in imitation of angels. In the liturgy of the new covenant, Christ himself presides, and we not only imitate the angels; we participate with them. Through the Mass—and in every Mass—there is *communion* between heaven and earth.

We can see that reality most vividly in the book of Revelation, where the Church on earth gathers at the altar with the angels and saints in heaven . . . where we hear the "Holy, Holy, Holy," the "Lamb of God," the Amen and Alleluia and other familiar songs . . . where priests serve in vestments in a sanctuary adorned with candles . . . where chalices are poured out and worshippers feast on "hidden manna." It is, I believe, no accident that the Apocalypse divides neatly into two halves, the first consisting of readings and the second of the "marriage supper of the Lamb." This structure corresponds to the most ancient order of divine worship.

For Christian liturgy still follows the basic pattern of Old Testament worship: a service that includes both the reading of the Word of God and the offering of sacrifice. Jesus himself followed that outline when he appeared to his disciples on the road to Emmaus: "Beginning with Moses and all the prophets, he interpreted to them in all the Scriptures the things concerning himself"; and then they knew him "in the breaking of the bread" (Lk 24:27, 35). In the Mass, we still hear the New Testament readings along with the Old Testament, and we view all the history of salvation in light of its ultimate fulfillment—in light of Christ. In the Mass, we still know Jesus, really present, in the breaking of the bread.

The New Covenant is indeed something new, great, and glorious. Yet we should not forget its continuity with the past. Israel's ritual worship was ordered to covenant remembrance (in reading) and renewal (in sacrifice). Christian worship, too, is a remembrance of God's mighty works in history, especially Jesus' saving passion and glorification. The Christian Eucharist remains both a covenant renewal and a thanksgiving for God's continued presence among his people.

Now that presence is a true communion. This fact astonished the early Christians, who proclaimed that the Mass was heaven on earth, and the earthly altar was the same as the heavenly. The Mass is the coming of Christ we all await. God comes to us in true communion, and the "marvelous exchange" takes on a flesh-and-blood dimension. We are God's children now, and "the children share in flesh and blood" (Heb 2:14).

This does not mean that the parishioners around us will remind us of Raphael's cherubs. Sometimes they'll have screaming babies with pungent diapers. It does not mean that the choir at St. Dymphna's Parish will ever sing on key. Nor does it mean Father's preaching will be consistently compelling.

It means what the incarnation has always meant: "the Word became flesh and dwelt among us" (Jn 1:14) . . . He "emptied himself" and "humbled himself" (Phil 2:7–8) . . . "the dwelling of God is with men. He will dwell with them, and they shall be his people, and God himself will be with them" (Rev 21:3).

In the Mass, he is "God with us" (Mt 1:23) where we are, as we are, though he loves us too much to leave us that way. Through the Eucharist, he makes us what he is; where he is he transforms us from glory to glory.

Ponder in Your Heart

Here we must apply our minds attentively, and consider the apostolic wisdom; for again he shows the change in the priesthood, who "serve a copy and shadow of the heavenly sanctuary" (Heb 8:5).

What are the heavenly things he speaks of here? The spiritual things. For although they are done on earth, yet nevertheless they are worthy of the heavens. For when our Lord Jesus Christ lies slain [as a sacrifice], when the Spirit is with us, when he who sits at the right hand of the Father is here, when sons are made by the washing, when they are fellow-citizens of those in heaven, when we have a country, and a city, and citizenship there, when we are strangers to things here, how can all these be other than heavenly things?

But what! Are not our hymns heavenly? Do not we also who are below utter together with them the same things that the divine choirs of bodiless powers sing above? Is not the altar also heavenly? How? It has nothing carnal, all spiritual things become the offerings. The sacrifice does not disperse into ashes, or into smoke, or into steamy savor, it makes the things placed there bright and splendid. How again can the rites that we celebrate be other than heavenly? For when he says, "If you forgive the sins of any, they are forgiven; if you retain the sins of any, they are retained" (Jn 20:23), when they have the keys of heaven, how can all be other than heavenly? . . .

No, one would not be wrong in saying even this; for the Church is heavenly, and is nothing else than heaven.

—St. John Chrysostom, fifth century

5.

Guardian Angels

Among the liveliest traditions in the ancient Church was devotion to the guardian angels. Yet it is something that modern readers often miss. The dramatic plot of the Acts of the Apostles is borne forward by the action of angels. Angels set the apostles free from prison (5:19, 12:7). An angel guides Philip from Jerusalem to Gaza for his fateful meeting with the Ethiopian court official (8:26). Angels bring about the meeting of Peter and Cornelius (10:3–5). My favorite instance is when Peter arrives at a house-church, and the people assume that it's *not* Peter, but rather his angel (12:15)!

The story of the Church moves forward with the guidance, protection, and assistance of angels. So do our lives. The early Christians knew this. That's why they could easily mistake a man for his guardian angel. Since Peter was imprisoned, they would naturally be surprised to find him at the door, but they were *not* surprised to encounter his angel!

We need to have such faith and such a lively awareness of our guardian angels. For God has given us—each of us—the same powerful heavenly guidance, protection, and assistance.

Devotion to the angels did not arise as something new with the proclamation of the Gospel. It has always been a part of biblical religion. Angels fill the Bible, from beginning to end, Genesis to Revelation. They are key players in the drama of the Garden of Eden. They appear frequently in the life of the patriarchs: Jacob even wrestles with one. They go before the Israelites during the exodus. They deliver God's word to the prophets. The prophets themselves reveal that even *nations* have guardian angels. The book of Tobit shows us how an angel guided a young man to recover his family's fortune, discover a cure for his father's blindness, and find a beautiful and virtuous wife along the way!

The New Testament opens with an explosion of angelic activity. Neither Joseph nor Mary seems particularly surprised to receive the help of angels.

What exactly are angels? The word comes from the Greek *angelos,* which is used to translate the Hebrew *malakh.* In those languages, the words denote, literally, a "messenger"—a messenger from God. In the great tradition the term *angel* has come to apply to the entire range of bodiless, purely spiritual beings created by God. Some he created for worship at his throne. Others he also gave the power of governance over the natural powers of the universe. Some are messengers. In the Bible, they sometimes appear in human form—or even in scarifying symbolic form, with many eyes (representing their prodigious knowledge) or titanic size (representing their superhuman strength).

As we saw in the last chapter, both Jews and Christians in the ancient world kept a healthy awareness of angelic presence *especially* during their ritual worship. It is interesting to note that one of the most popular books in the community that preserved the Dead Sea Scrolls was a manual for worship called *The Angelic Liturgy.*

Still today, when we go to Mass, the congregation is never small, even if it is *nonexistent* in terms of human attendance. The angels are there, as is evident even in the words of the Mass: "And so with all the choirs of angels we sing: Holy, holy, holy . . ." The Mass itself cries out for us to be aware of our angels.

We should, of course, be particularly attentive to our own guardian angels, since they are specifically assigned to our care.

Devotion to the angels is sure to raise a condescending smile from rationalists, who will reduce it to sentimental holy cards depicting little children on a rickety bridge. Yet angels have always been part of biblical religion; and, as even secular philosophers have acknowledged, it's hard to account for the cosmos without them. The twentieth-century liberal philosopher Isaiah Berlin was fairly obsessed with the necessity of angels. The philosopher Mortimer Adler was a self-described "pagan" when he concluded that angels were part of the fabric of the universe.

If we could see things as they are, and not merely as they appear, we would find it hard to account for our lives without some understanding of the place of angels.

From the time we are smallest, each of us has a guardian angel. Jesus said: "See that you do not despise one of these little ones; for I tell you that in heaven their angels always behold the face of my Father who is in heaven" (Mt 18:10).

God gives us these guides so that we may have superhuman help on our way to heaven. Our guardian angels want to help us cooperate with the will of God, and they want to keep us from sinning. They want to help us to help others—and they want to keep us from mucking up the lives of others. Along the way, of course, they may help us to walk safely across an unsteady bridge, but only if that will accomplish God's will for us and for the world. They want the best for us, which does not always coincide with the things we desire most. The difficult fact is that what's best for us does not necessarily correspond with our comfort, health, or safety. Sometimes suffering is what's best for us, if only because it keeps us from sinning or tempting others to sin.

Still, our guardian angels do work diligently to win our trust—because that indeed is in *our* own best interest. And so they do undoubtedly help us, especially when we ask them, to find an open parking space or navigate a confusing grid of city streets. The angels follow after God's pattern of governance: they sometimes give us what we want so that we'll learn to ask for what we need.

Always remember: we are God's children now. No one spends as much on child care as God does. Why does he lavish so much on us, creating powerful pure spirits to watch over us?

Because he loves us, of course, and because he has called us all to holiness—a state that means more than mere "goodness." To be holy is to be set apart for a divine purpose, to be set apart for God. God made the Garden of Eden to be a holy place, and he positioned angels to guard it and keep it pure (Gen 3:24). When he commissioned the tabernacle and later the Jerusalem Temple, he intended these places to be his sanctuaries, and he positioned angels to guard them (Ex 25:18; I Kgs 8:6–7).

We were created to be not a random collection of carbon, hydrogen, and oxygen molecules, but as temples of the Holy Spirit (I Cor 3:16, 6:19). Our angels, like those primeval cherubim, are charged with the task of protecting the sanctuary and keeping it pure for the presence of God.

We would do well often to pray the rhyme that's taught to little children:

Angel of God, my guardian dear,
To whom God's love commits me here:
Ever this day be at my side
To light and guard, to rule and guide. Amen.

We should also know the protection of St. Michael the Archangel. He appears in Scripture as the special guardian of God's people in the Old Testament (Dan 12:1) and the New (Rev 12:7). The Church has always recognized St. Michael's role in the spiritual combat. He is invoked as a warrior against the devil and all rebel angels. Prayer to St. Michael is especially powerful when we need deliverance from evil. For many years this traditional "St. Michael Prayer" was recited at the end of the Mass. Many, many Catholics retain it as part of their regular devotions:

> St. Michael the Archangel, defend us in battle. Be our protection against the wickedness and snares of the devil. May God rebuke him, we humbly pray. And do thou, O prince of the heavenly host, by the power of God, cast into hell Satan and all other evil spirits who prowl about the world seeking the ruin of souls. Amen.

Ponder in Your Heart

Let us look for a moment at this appearance of angels in Jesus' life, for it will help us to better understand their role—their angelic mission—in all human life. Christian tradition describes the guardian angels as powerful friends, placed by God alongside each one of us, to accompany us on our way. And that is why he invites us to make friends with them and get them to help us . . .

We have to fill ourselves with courage, for the grace of God will not fail us. God will be at our side and will send his angels to be our traveling companions, our prudent advisers along the way, our cooperators in all that we take on. The angels "will hold you up with their hands lest you should chance to trip on a stone," as the psalm says.

We must learn to speak to the angels. Turn to them now . . . Ask them to take up to the Lord your good will, which, by the grace of God, has grown out of your wretchedness like a lily grown on a dunghill. Holy angels, our guardians: "defend us in battle so that we do not perish at the final judgment."

—St. Josemaría Escrivá, twentieth century

II

Life Times

6.

The Church's Calendar

Rabbi Samson Raphael Hirsch, considered by many to be the founder of modern Orthodox Judaism, spoke poetically about the religious importance of the calendar.

> The catechism of the Jew consists of his calendar. On the pinions of time which bear us through life, God has inscribed the eternal words of His soul-inspiring doctrine, making days and weeks, months and years the heralds to proclaim His truths. Nothing would seem more fleeting than these elements of time, but to them God has entrusted the care of His holy things, thereby rendering them more imperishable and more accessible.

Everything he said about the Jewish calendar could be applied just as well to the Christian year. Though we Catholics *do* have a catechism (and thank God for that!), we often learn our doctrine much more deeply and effectively simply by celebrating the feasts and fasts of the Church. In fact, the *Catechism of the Catholic Church* itself begins to wax poetic when it speaks of the calendar as a year-long teaching moment. "The cycle of the liturgical year and its great feasts are . . . basic rhythms of the Christian's life of prayer" (CCC, n. 2698). The great feasts "commemorate" and "communicate" the mystery of Christ (n. 1171). They are an invitation to *regular* prayer, intended to nourish *continual* prayer (nn. 2720, 2698).

"Counting the days" is an integral part of what we do and who we are. It's human nature. We mark anniversaries and birthdays. We celebrate milestones. We define ourselves by those dates and spans. I am fifty-one years old today. I have been married for twenty-nine years. I have been a Catholic for twenty-two years. I have been teaching in the same place for eighteen years. I can tell you the birth date of each of my children and grandchildren.

My professional life is similarly marked off by semesters and midterms. A professor's year follows a certain rhythm, as does a farmer's and a tax accountant's. It's our nature to mark time this way, to number our days aright.

No one knows human nature better than the God who created it. That's why he fashioned the world to follow certain rhythms. The book of Genesis tells us that the Lord God made the world in six days and rested on the seventh. He rested not because he was weary—almighty God does not grow tired—but because he wanted to provide a model for human labor and human rest. Ever after, his people knew that they should work six days that were oriented to the seventh, the Sabbath. Their days of work were directed toward a day to worship the Lord in freedom. When they failed to follow this rhythm, he codified it as law, so that they should always "remember the Sabbath day, to keep it holy" (Ex 20:8).

The sacred calendar coincided with the cosmic rhythms. The feasts in the Old Testament marked not only sacred and historic events, but also seedtime and harvest. The Law concerned itself not only with the tenure of priests in the tabernacle, but also with the phases of human fertility.

The sacred calendar kept time with the cosmic rhythms, but the cosmic rhythms themselves were there to provide a haven for holiness.

Jesus was keenly aware of the calendar and its religious significance, as were his disciples. Remember how earnestly he desired to eat the Passover with the Twelve (see Lk 22:15). Notice how faithfully he and his family—and later his band of disciples—made pilgrimage to Jerusalem at the appointed times. When St. John wrote his account of Jesus' ministry, he carefully recorded that the drama had unfolded according to the calendar of Jewish feasts. In its climactic scene, Jesus died on the cross at precisely the moment when the Passover lambs were sacrificed in the Temple.

When the Word became flesh, all creation and all history found its fulfillment. The doctrine of God came into sharper focus, suddenly revealed *in person.* The calendar itself reflects this fact. Gradually, the months and days reordered themselves—actually, God's people reordered them—to teach the Gospel in its fullness. Thus, all of human time coalesced around the resurrection of Jesus Christ. The week no longer led to Sabbath, but to Sunday, the Lord's Day, the day on which Jesus rose from the dead. The year still culminated in the Passover, but now the *Christian Passover,* which is the feast of salvation through the Lord's passion, death, and resurrection.

The Lord's Day and Easter were the two primary holy days of the newborn Church. Gradually, though, believers added new feasts: the baptism of the Lord, his conception, his birth, his ascension, and so on.

The Church marked off not only the days of his life, but of our life today. For Jesus is the "pioneer of our faith" (Heb 12:2). He is the "firstborn of many brethren" (Rom 8:29). Those terms imply that others, many others, are to follow; and so the Church proved this claim by celebrating the feasts of the saints, beginning with the Blessed Virgin Mary, but including the apostles, martyrs, and many others.

The year, as it has developed, is, like a microscope or telescope, a finely tuned instrument for keeping its object always in focus, always near; and its object is Jesus Christ.

The Christian calendar, like the Jewish calendar, counts units of days, weeks, and months. It has Holy Week and many "octaves," which are eight-day spans, some devoted to biblical mysteries like Easter and Pentecost, but others devoted to prayer intentions like Christian unity. The Christian calendar has seasons like Lent and Advent, Easter and Christmas, as well as "ordinary time." The Church also keeps the custom of reserving months—May for Mary and October for her Rosary. For those who pray the Rosary, every day brings a different set of mysteries for meditation, in the cycle of joy, light, sorrow, and glory. As someone once sang: "To everything there is a season, and a time for every purpose under heaven" (Eccl 3:1). Every now and then, the pope will even choose an entire year out of the stream of history and denote it a "Holy Year."

In the course of the liturgical year, Christians receive repeated exposure to the major events of salvation history. The lectionary orders the Church's readings—Old Testament foreshadowing and New Testament fulfillment—for proclamation at Mass. The celebration of the other rites—sacraments and sacramentals—applies the same pattern to the course of a lifetime. Because of the lectionary's unfolding, the weeks, the seasons, and the years tell a unified, continuous story and, in the process, teach doctrine.

The cycle brings times of fasting and times of feasting, times of sorrow and times of joy, times of penance and times of reconciliation. All creation tells the story. All history tells the story. All our lives, yours and mine, tell the story.

It is a story of hope. It is our "strong encouragement to seize the hope set before us . . . a hope that enters into the inner shrine behind the curtain" (Heb 6:18–19).

Ponder in Your Heart

People are instructed in the truths of faith, and brought to appreciate the inner joys of religion, far more effectually by the annual celebration of our sacred mysteries than by any official pronouncement of the teaching of the Church. Such pronouncements usually reach only a few and the more learned among the faithful; feasts reach them all; the former speak but once, the latter speak every year—in fact, forever. The Church's teaching affects the mind primarily; her feasts affect both mind and heart, and have a salutary effect upon the whole of man's nature. Man is composed of body and soul, and he needs these external festivities so that the sacred rites, in all their beauty and variety, may stimulate him to drink more deeply of the fountain of God's teaching, that he may make it a part of himself, and use it with profit for his spiritual life.

History, in fact, tells us that in the course of ages these festivals have been instituted one after another according as the needs or the advantage of the people of Christ seemed to demand: as when they needed strength to face a common danger, when they were attacked by insidious heresies, when they needed to be urged to the pious consideration of some mystery of faith or of some divine blessing.

—Pope Pius XI, twentieth century

7.

LENT AND EASTER

We who speak English suffer a fundamental disorientation when we consider the central mysteries of faith. In most languages, the same word applies to the Jewish Passover as to the Christian feast of Jesus' resurrection. It is *Pascua, Pascha, Pasqua, Pesach, Πάσχα*. The English name, on the other hand, derives from an ancient German spring festival, about which we know very little today.

Thus the term "Paschal Mystery" doesn't have quite the same associations for us as it has for others. It is this mystery, according to the *Catechism,* that "stands at the center" of the Gospel (CCC, n. 571). All the other feasts, all the other mysteries point to the central mystery we celebrate at Easter (CCC, n. 1171). Yet it is the same Paschal Mystery that we celebrate every Sunday, and indeed in every Mass. We may think of these memorials as widening concentric circles, whose heart is the Lord's saving passion.

For Christians, the Paschal Mystery should evoke the ancient Passover, when all the firstborn children of Israel were spared, when the chosen people were liberated from slavery, and when they embarked upon their journey to the promised land. Their deliverance began, in each household, with the sacrifice of a lamb and the smearing of the lamb's blood on the doorposts. In future generations, Jews would recall those saving events, but would also consider them allegorically, as God's continued deliverance of his people, out of vice and into virtue.

In the fullness of time, Jesus came as the "Lamb of God" (Jn 1:29). For his disciples he was "Christ, our paschal lamb," who "has been sacrificed" (I Cor 5:7). For Christians, the Passover has not been abolished, but rather fulfilled. "Let us, therefore," said St. Paul, "celebrate the festival, not with the old leaven, the leaven of malice and evil, but with the unleavened bread of sincerity and truth" (I Cor 5:8).

Raised up in the traditions of Judaism, the first Christians could see both the continuity and discontinuity from the Old Covenant to the New. They still celebrated the festival with unleavened bread, but now the sacrifice was Christ himself, who had made an explicit offering of his body at the Last Supper. It was that moment, that paschal meal, that transformed his execution into a once-for-all sacrifice.

The Old Testament Passover began with Israel's redemption of the firstborn and liberation from slavery, but it culminated much later with the people's entrance into the promised land, "a land flowing with milk and honey" (Jos 5:6). Between those events, the tribes wandered in the desert for forty years. Those years were a time of purification, when God purged the Israelites of the residual effects of generations of contact with Egyptian idolatry.

That pattern played itself out in Jesus' own life. Before he launched his public ministry—inaugurating his kingdom—he fasted and prayed for forty days in the wilderness. He did this even though he was sinless and had no need of purification. His fast was, like his baptism, a model for his disciples to imitate.

So, every year, as we prepare to celebrate Easter, the great feast
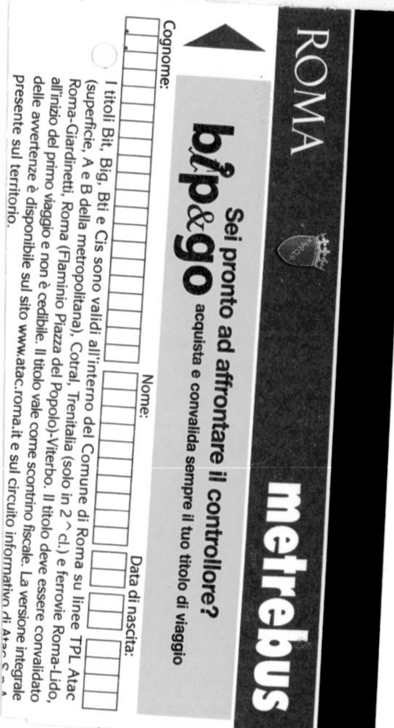

dergo purification through forty days
Lent. Lent is the season that begins
s on Holy Saturday, the day before
undays (the ancient Fathers forbade
ally makes for a total of forty days.

arily symbolic—and it is richly sym-
we have to a forty-day preparation for
e Council of Nicaea (A.D. 325). One
sions of its meaning, however, appears
sian in the fifth century. He describes
ar," because it is roughly a tenth of the
days to the Lord as a special offering;
his own fast, as he intended us to do.
d Testament models of Israel in the
and Elijah, who also underwent forty-
day fast.

If we are lay people living in the world, we need not take on a monastic fast of bread and water. In my country, we follow the Lenten custom of fasting by "giving something up," preferably a favorite food or pastime to which we are unduly attached. We may also stop eating between meals, or skip dessert, or forgo second helpings. We return it all to God for forty days, not because any of it is "bad," but because it is indeed very good. Only good things should be offered in sacrifice to God; only the best of the harvest could be offered as a tithe. We give them to God so that we learn not to put anything in God's place in our lives.

It goes without saying that we should also give up any habits that are sinful and immoral—but these are not normally the stuff of a Lenten fast. They're actions to be renounced (at least in our intentions) even before we begin the disciplines of Lent.

Fasting, we prepare ourselves for the feast. In the words of St. Athanasius: "purified by the fast of forty days, by prayers, and fastings, and discipline, and good works, we shall be able to eat the holy Passover in Jerusalem." Now that Christ is our Passover and he has ascended, we celebrate the feast, not in the earthly Jerusalem, but in a new holy city. "But you have come to Mount Zion and to the city of the living God, the heavenly Jerusalem, and to innumerable angels in festal gathering, and to the assembly of the first-born who are enrolled in heaven, and to a judge who is God of all, and to the spirits of just men made perfect, and to Jesus, the mediator of a new covenant, and to the sprinkled blood that speaks more graciously than the blood of Abel" (Heb 12:22–24).

Thus the early Church celebrated the Easter Mass with special solemnity. In some places, the celebration lasted the entire night, from sundown on Easter Vigil till sunrise on Easter morning. In the course of the liturgy, the Church read selected passages from Scripture that told the story of salvation in rough outline, from creation through the flood, from the vocation of Abraham through the exodus, from the kingdom of David to the exile—culminating in the mystery of Christ. This is why in the Gospels' remembrance of the passion we find a reprise of all the major themes of the Old Testament. We find allusions to the Garden of Eden, the flood tide that washed the earth, the offering of the firstborn Isaac, the slaughter of the lamb. All of history is caught up now in the great Paschal Mystery.

The ancient liturgy of Easter Vigil was still more than that. It was not just a liturgy of the word, but of baptism and Eucharist. Easter Vigil was when new Christians were welcomed into the mysteries of faith, sometimes after years of intensive preparation. The life of the world, the life of the Church, and the lives of so many individuals were now arriving at their dramatic climax. A second-century bishop put it this way in his homily for Easter Vigil: "The Law became the Word, the old became the new . . . the model became the reality, the lamb became the Son."

The climax of *everything* is baptism, which the early Church called "illumination" or "enlightenment" (Heb 6:4, 10:32), and then Eucharist, which the apostles knew as a *koinonia*, or "communion."

From ancient times, the Church saw the Christian pilgrimage as a movement from *purification* to *illumination* and finally to *union* with God. These are the stages we mark as we pass through the sacraments of initiation. They trace a pattern that plays itself out over the course of history, over the course of a lifetime, over the course of the liturgical week, over the course of a year, and even over the course of the Mass.

We "pass over" from sin through penance to communion as we conform ourselves to the Easter mysteries.

Ponder in Your Heart

We firmly believe, brethren, that the Lord has died for our sins . . . All of that happened once and for all, as you know well enough. And yet we have the liturgical solemnities which we celebrate as, during the course of the year, we come to the date of particular events. Between the truth of the events and the solemnities of the liturgy there is no contradiction, as if the latter were a lie. The historical truth is what happened once and for all, but the liturgy makes those events always new for the hearts that celebrate them with faith. The historical truth shows us the events just as they happened, but the liturgy, while not repeating them, celebrates them and prevents them from being forgotten. Thus, on the basis of historical truth, we say that Easter happened once only and will not happen again, but, on the basis of the liturgy, we can say that Easter happens every year. Thanks to the liturgy, the human mind reaches the truth and proclaims its faith in the Lord.

—St. Augustine of Hippo, fourth century

8.

Advent and Christmas

Christmas is a day and a season that requires no introduction, right? From the day after Halloween, the media and the storefronts relentlessly remind us of the holiday's imminence. The festival of Jesus' birth is the reason for the peak sales season in a retailer's year. Economists monitor it closely and analyze it endlessly as an indicator of the nation's financial health.

And I don't want to begrudge them a penny of it. Let the Grinches and Scrooges mutter darkly about the commercialization of Christmas. I'll take it (though not uncritically) as a tribute to Christ that society's great season of giving is the feast of his birth, even if that giving must be preceded by a season of buying.

I do, however, grieve for the eclipse of Advent; for the Church's season of spiritual preparation for Christmas has certainly been overwhelmed by the ever-expanding "Christmas shopping season." Advent is a season we must recover, even if it takes heroic effort.

In Advent the liturgy bids us to relive the period of expectation when the world awaited the Savior. We hear the words of the prophets, and we make them our own. The prophets longed for the conditions that Israel could only enjoy upon faithful fulfillment of the covenant. Instead, the people fell inexorably into sin, and so they lost the privileges God had given them: prosperity and happiness in a land flowing with milk and honey. The prophets ached for a messiah, ached for a redeemer, ached for a deliverer.

With the birth of Jesus came the fulfillment of all the holy desires of all those many centuries. That is the joy we mark in Christmas, but it's difficult for us to experience the joy unless we first undergo the longing.

That is why the Church leads us first through a season not of shopping, *but of longing.* Advent is sometimes called "the little Lent," because it is a season of preparatory fasting and self-denial. It is not as long as "Great Lent." In fact, it can be as short as twenty-one days. Yet it still should be a time of some small, daily sacrifices. The apostles fasted to prepare for worship in the Lord's presence (Acts 13:2). We should, too. That empty feeling should serve as a sensible sign of our spiritual need.

It is good for us, at least once a year, to recall the pain and poverty of a world without Christ. For centuries now, we have lived in a world shaped by Christian assumptions—Christian notions of right and wrong, of decency, of justice, and of human dignity. Now, as the world forgets Christ, all these natural benefits of his advent are vanishing as well. In post-Christian states, we have seen the notion of human dignity fade to non-existence, followed soon by human rights, beginning with the right to life. In a post-Christian world, we have seen ethnic minorities emerging anew—and violently—to wage brutal separatist wars against their closest cousins. The world is rapidly losing any sense of the transnational family Christ came to inaugurate, the kingdom where Israel and the Gentiles can live together in peace.

If we want to hold fast to the good things that came with Christ, then we must first keep a lively remembrance of the difference Christ made—the difference Christmas made. Advent calls us out of our cultural complacency. The Church echoes the prophets, who say: "Woe to those who are at ease in Zion" (Am 6:1), that is, those who have taken God's extraordinary gifts for granted.

If we are tempted to grumble about a culture that has forgotten Christ, then perhaps we are beginning to sense the longing of the prophets.

Christ has come, and yet we await him anew. He has saved us, and yet we still await a day when "he will wipe away every tear . . . and death shall be no more, neither shall there be mourning nor crying nor pain any more" (Rev 21:4). Christ has come, and he continues to come to us in the Eucharist. But he will come again, at the consummation of history. For this day, even the souls of the just in heaven cry out, "How long?" as did the ancient prophets (see Rev 6:10).

Advent reminds us that there are still two dimensions to our salvation: "already" and "not yet." In Advent we sing the ancient songs of longing and expectation, the "O Antiphons," because we await our Savior's coming in fullness, his "plenary parousia," as the theologians call it. When he comes at the end of time, he will have no more glory than he has now in the Eucharist, but then we'll see him as he is. The difference will be not with him, but with us: "we know that when he appears . . . we shall see him as he is" (1 Jn 3:2). Thus we hope for that day, and we fast through Advent, because, as we read in the very next line of St. John's letter: "everyone who thus hopes in him purifies himself as he is pure."

A blessed Advent, then, is the only true key to a merry Christmas. Christians should never be like the segments of affluent society that a social critic called "souls without longing." We should know longing habitually, because we have practiced longing at least annually, during Advent.

Advent is a time of vigilance, alertness, expectation. We are eager for the arrival of Christ, so we pay close attention to our life of prayer, our moral life, the way we treat others, and the way we express our love for God. We should not allow ourselves to experience "Xmas fatigue" long before December 25 rolls around. We should, if necessary, fast from the radio so that we don't hear an endless round of misplaced seasonal carols beginning the day after Thanksgiving, or fast from television programming that anticipates Christmas fulfillment during Advent's waiting. We should also show others that it is possible to buy for Christmas without bowing idolatrously to commercialism.

The Church is a refuge from a premature nativity. Catholic churches feel different during Advent (or they should). In the Mass, we eliminate the Gloria, because that is a Christmas song, the chant of the angels at the birth in Bethlehem (Lk 2:14). In fact, choirs and musicians are supposed to refrain from using *any* Christmas music during Advent liturgies.

Hope is the reason for the season, and Jesus Christ is certainly worth the wait. We could not reasonably expect a better Christmas present than Simeon and Anna received during that first octave of Christmas (Lk 2:25–38). They had waited long lives, not merely four weeks. Think, too, of the magi, who had scanned the skies in hope, looking for a sign.

We know him "already," but still "not yet." So let's keep our days as we should, looking for signs and then rejoicing in the mystery of the incarnation.

Ponder in Your Heart

Advent is celebrated for four weeks, to signify that this coming of the Lord is fourfold; namely, that he came to us in the flesh, that he came with mercy into our hearts, that he came to us in death, and that he will come to us again at the Last Judgment. The last week is seldom finished, to denote that the glory of the elect, as they will receive it at the last advent of the Lord, will have no end. But while the coming is in reality fourfold, the Church is especially concerned with two of its forms, namely with the coming in the flesh and with the coming at the Last Judgment. Thus the Advent fast is both a joyous fast, and a fast of penance. It is a joyous fast because it recalls the advent of the Lord in the flesh; and it is a fast of penance in anticipation of the advent of the Last Judgment.

With regard to the advent in the flesh, three things should be considered: its timeliness, its necessity, and its usefulness. Its timeliness is due first to the fact that man, condemned by his nature to an imperfect knowledge of God, had fallen into the worst errors of idolatry, and was forced to cry out, "Enlighten my eyes." Secondly, the Lord came in the "fullness of time," as St. Paul says in the Epistle to the Galatians. Thirdly, He came at a time when the whole world was ailing, as St. Augustine says: "The great physician came at a moment when the entire world lay like a great invalid." That is why the Church, in the seven antiphons that are sung before the Feast of the Nativity, recalls the variety of our ills and the timeliness of the divine remedy. Before the coming of God in the flesh, we were ignorant, subject to eternal punishment, slaves of the devil, shackled with sinful habits, lost in darkness, exiled from our true country. Hence the ancient antiphons announce Jesus in turn as our Teacher, our Redeemer, our Liberator, our Guide, our Enlightener, and our Savior.

As to the usefulness of Christ's coming, different authorities define it differently. Our Lord Himself, in the Gospel of Saint Luke, tells us that He came for seven reasons to console the poor, to heal the afflicted, to free the captives, to enlighten the ignorant, to pardon sinners, to redeem the human race, and to reward everyone according to his merits. And . . . St. Bernard says, "We suffer from a three-fold sickness: we are easily misled, weak in action, and feeble in resistance. Consequently the coming of the Lord is necessary, first to enlighten our blindness, second to succor our weakness, and third to shield our fragility."

—Jacobus de Voragine, thirteenth century

9.

NOVENAS

Novenas are certainly among the most popular forms of devotion in modern times. They have ancient roots, even strong biblical roots. Yet their current forms, and their current wave of popularity, are relatively recent in Church terms—that is, they date back "only" to the 1600s.

A novena is a prayer that involves nine steps. It may involve nine prayers to be recited over a certain period. Or it may require the same prayer to be repeated nine times—for example, daily over nine days or weekly over nine weeks.

The word comes from the Latin *novem,* which means nine. Devotees trace the practice back to the day of the ascension, when Jesus initiated nine days of prayer: "he charged them not to depart from Jerusalem, but to wait for the promise of the Father . . . and when they had entered, they went up to the upper room, where they were staying . . . All these with one accord devoted themselves to prayer, together with the women and Mary the mother of Jesus"

(Acts 1:4–14). For nine days the disciples prayed, and on the tenth day, Pentecost, they received the Holy Spirit.

The early Church observed other nine-day devotions. Grieving families and friends would observe nine days of prayer or Masses, with almsgiving, offered for the repose of deceased loved ones.

What is significant about the number nine? Some commentators have suggested that it is one short of ten, a round number that represents fullness and perfection, so it is a sign of our human neediness, our imperfection. Since we often pray novenas for special intentions, this is an interpretation that corresponds to reality.

There are many novenas in circulation, and we are free to offer our own favorite prayers in bundles of nine. But the Church recommends that we try to key our private devotions to the liturgical year—because, as pointed out earlier, the calendar is a catechism, and we should respect the logic of its unfolding. Thus, the novenas most popular with the popes have always clustered around major feast days. Pope Leo XIII decreed, in his encyclical letter on the Holy Spirit (*Divinum Illud Munus*) that every Catholic parish should observe an annual novena to the Holy Spirit, in imitation of the apostles and the Blessed Virgin, on the days between Ascension and Pentecost.

All the recent popes have shown a special fondness for the "Christmas novena"—nine days of prayers or meditations leading up to the feast of the Nativity. Each day represents one of the months that Jesus dwelt in his mother's womb. Pope Benedict XVI has wished that all Catholics would live the spirit of this devotion: "In the Christmas Novena . . . as we gradually draw close to the Holy Night, the liturgy, increasing in spiritual intensity, makes us repeat: '*Maranatha!* Come, Lord Jesus!' This invocation rises from the hearts of believers in all corners of the earth and ceaselessly resounds in every Ecclesial Community." There is nothing to stop us from taking up this medieval observance this year, with those simple words "*Maranatha!* Come, Lord Jesus!" recited once daily for nine days (see 1 Cor 16:22; Rev 22:20).

The popes and recent saints have also been fond of the Immaculate Conception novena, which can help believers prepare for this great feast day of the Blessed Virgin.

Novenas are best keyed to liturgical feasts, but they need not always be. We often pray novenas for needs that arise in the course of life. Blessed Pope John XXIII, on the eve of the Second Vatican Council, begged all the parishes in the world to offer a solemn novena to the Holy Spirit. Sometimes our need for an outpouring of the Holy Spirit, like his, doesn't quite correspond to the Church's calendar!

Blessed Mother Teresa of Calcutta, in moments of dire need, taught her sisters to pray an "express novena"—nine repetitions of the beloved Marian prayer, the Memorare:

> Remember, O most gracious Virgin Mary, that never was it known that anyone who fled to your protection, implored your help, or sought your intercession was left unaided. Inspired by this confidence, I fly unto you, O Virgin of virgins, my mother; to you do I come, before you I stand, sinful and sorrowful. O Mother of the Word Incarnate, despise not my petitions, but in your mercy hear and answer me. Amen.

Mother Teresa reported many favors received after the conclusion of these novenas (which are also popularly called "storm novenas," because they "storm heaven").

As we pray novenas, it's good for us to remember the fundamentals of Christian prayer. We go to God in our need; we raise our minds and hearts to him; and we ask him for good things. We should take care not to treat prayer as a mechanical or magical action. We're not out to change God's mind; God does not change. Quite the contrary: prayer is God's favorite way of changing *our* minds. This is not to deny that prayer is efficacious. As I said in an earlier chapter, God sometimes gives us what we want so that we'll grow in our trust and learn to ask him for what we need.

It is fashionable in certain circles to sneer at popular devotion, but that's something I never want to do. I've learned over the years that simple faith often runs much deeper than graduate-level theology courses.

Still, I have received enough novenas via e-mail and picked up enough photocopies in the back of the church to know that a word of caution is in order. It pains me deeply when someone publishes what they call a "never-fail novena." There is a sense, of course, in which every novena is fail-safe. God hears every prayer, and he answers every prayer, and he answers every prayer with our best interests in mind. The phrase "never-fail" suggests, however, that God can somehow be managed or manipulated, and it can create a crisis of faith for those who believe it's a guarantee that they'll get what they want, just the way they want it. Already in the second century, the North African writer Tertullian was worrying about Christians whose prayer had veered into superstition—little different from the pagan approach. Instead of seeking to align themselves with the will of God, they looked upon prayers as ways to manipulate the deity. We should take care not to pray this way or promote prayer that could mislead people who are poorly instructed in the faith. "Never-fail" is best kept for peanut-butter fudge recipes, not novenas!

Ponder in Your Heart

The Acts of the Apostles reminds us of the period after Christ's Ascension into Heaven, when the Apostles, at his command, returned to the Upper Room and remained there in prayer with the Mother of Jesus and the brothers and sisters of the primitive community which was the first nucleus of the Church (cf. 1:12–14). Each year, after the Ascension, the Church relives this first novena, the novena to the Holy Spirit. The apostles, gathered in the Upper Room with the Mother of Christ, pray for the accomplishment of the promise made to them by the Risen Christ: "You shall receive power when the Holy Spirit has come upon you; and you shall be my witnesses" (1:8). This first apostolic novena to the Holy Spirit is the model of what the Church does each year.

The Church prays: *Veni, Creator Spiritus!*

"Come, Creator Spirit, visit the souls of your people,
Fill with grace from on high the hearts which you have created . . ."

I am moved as I repeat this prayer of the Universal Church with you . . . We are confident: the Holy Spirit will renew the face of the earth.

—Pope John Paul II, twentieth century

III

A Day in the Life

10.

Posture

My friend Msgr. George Kelly liked to brag a little bit about his mother. When she was very old, she required some surgery on an ailing leg. As her doctor ran through the options, explaining the trade-offs of each in terms of lingering pain and limitations on mobility, she grew visibly impatient. At the first opportunity, she cut the lecture short. And she informed him of her only real criterion for making the decision. He should fix her leg, she said, so that she could still genuflect—kneel briefly on her right knee—whenever she passed a tabernacle.

Mrs. Kelly knew, as the Psalmist knew, that posture matters. "O Lord, you have searched me and known me! You know when I sit down and when I rise up; you discern my thoughts from afar" (Ps 139:1–2). We are composed of body and soul and, as Romano Guardini put it, "every part of the body is an expressive instrument of the soul. The soul does not inhabit the body as a man inhabits a house. It lives and works in each member, each fiber, and reveals itself in the body's every line, contour, and movement."

Thus the soul expresses itself in our prayer, whether private or liturgical, not only by our words but by our gestures and by the way we comport ourselves. If we were invited to dinner at the White House or Buckingham Palace, it's unlikely that we would slouch, or stand with our hands in our pockets. Our bodies would communicate what we believe about the office of the president or monarch. Our bodies would communicate respect.

The Bible speaks of several postures of prayer: standing, kneeling, bowing, and prostration. The Church uses all of them at different and appropriate times.

In prostration, an individual lies face down upon the floor, with body and arms fully extended. Prostrations are reserved for most solemn moments, such as the ordination of a bishop or priest and the opening of the service on Good Friday. In the first case, the posture indicates the candidate's inadequacy for the task to which he has been called. In the second case, as Cardinal Ratzinger said poetically, the posture signifies the Church's "shock at the fact that we by our sins share in the responsibility for the death of Christ."

In Eastern Catholic parishes, I have seen altar servers prostrate themselves before the altar during the eucharistic prayer, the Anaphora. It is, there, a sign of profound reverence for Jesus, truly present in the Eucharist.

We may prostrate ourselves in private prayer as well, as I did before the steel cross on the night I recounted in this book's introduction. That gesture was, for me, an expression of the helplessness I was feeling, and of my own attempt to imitate Jesus, who, in his desolation and self-emptying, "fell on his face and prayed" (Mt 26:39).

Kneeling is another Gospel practice that we incorporate into the body language of our prayer life. In the New Testament, kneeling is the prayer posture of mothers, rulers, lepers, and Jesus himself (see Mt 8:2, 9:18, 15:25; Lk 22:41). St. Paul is pleased to say: "I bow my knees before the Father" (Eph 3:14).

But standing, too, gives expression to the prayers of our heart. Here's Father Guardini again: "Standing is the other side of reverence toward God. Kneeling is the side of worship in rest and quietness; standing is the side of vigilance and action. It is the respect of the servant in attendance, of the soldier on duty. When the good news of the gospel is proclaimed, we stand up . . . Bridegroom and bride stand when they bind themselves at the altar to be faithful to their marriage vow."

Yet we spend much of our liturgy neither kneeling nor standing—and certainly not prostrate. For the readings from the Old Testament, for example, we sit down. This, however, is hardly a neutral posture. When we sit, we assume a receptive position. We are listening, taking in the Word of God.

In prayer, every traditional posture is rich in meaning, as is every gesture. Consider the way we hold our hands, or fold them, in prayer. The fashions for this have changed down the centuries, and varied from place to place; but each development communicated something important. A knight with his hands together, for example, rendered himself vulnerable. He could not reach for a weapon. So he stood when he approached a king or judge. It was at once a sign of deference and trust. We, too, are "vulnerable" when we are in God's presence; for none of our weapons can harm him, and none of our defenses can repel him. We defer to him as greater than any earthly king, because he alone is all-powerful and all-knowing.

Hands pressed together, palm to palm, resemble a flame pointed heavenward—an appropriate image as we heed St. Paul's counsel to "present your bodies as a living sacrifice, holy and acceptable to God, which is your spiritual worship" (Rom 12:1).

Military officers know that comportment has serious consequences. Soldiers tend to live up, or live down, to the way they carry themselves. That's why there are strict rules about how a soldier should stand when at attention—or even "at ease"! Bad posture is not only bad for the spine; it's demoralizing—it brings down morale among the troops. It communicates disrespect not only for ourselves, but also for the others (or Other) present with us.

Care for gesture and posture, on the other hand, enables us to pray in an integrated way, "with heart and hands and voices." When we pray together with the Church, of course, as we do in the Mass, we should always move as the Church directs us: sit, stand, bow, kneel, strike the breast, make the Sign of the Cross, all in due time.

As Christians, we know we are not "ghosts in a machine." We are ensouled bodies as much as we are embodied souls. We are creatures composed of body and soul in an integral unity. Pope John Paul II was able to build an entire "Theology of the Body" out of the premise that the body expresses the "personal human self." Needless to say, that has profound consequences for the way we worship. Prayer is not just a matter of the mind. Still less is it mind over matter. It's all about all God has given us.

Ponder in Your Heart

The physical postures assumed during the Eucharistic Celebration—whether standing, sitting or kneeling—

express the attitudes of our hearts. Thus, the community at prayer transmits a whole spectrum of sentiments and dispositions.

The posture of standing expresses the filial liberty given us by the risen Christ, who has freed us from slavery to sin. That of sitting expresses the open-hearted receptiveness of Mary, who sat at the feet of Jesus to hear his word. And finally, the posture of kneeling or of bowing low expresses the recognition of our humility before the Almighty Lord (cf. Phil 2:10).

When the priest and the faithful genuflect before the Eucharist, they express their faith in the real presence of Jesus Christ in the sacrament of the altar.

By reflecting here below, by means of sacred signs, that liturgy celebrated in the heavenly sanctuary, we imitate the heavenly host, who "fall down before the one who sits on the throne and worship him, who lives forever and ever" (Rev 4:10).

If we adore the God who is "with us and for us" in the Eucharistic celebration, this spiritual attitude should prolong itself throughout the day in all we think and do. The ever-insidious temptation in managing the affairs of this world is to bend our knees before other idols, and not only before God.

Jesus' words in rejecting the devil's temptations in the desert should become our own pattern of thought, speech and action: "The Lord, your God, shall you worship and him alone shall you serve" (Mt 4:10).

In kneeling before the Eucharist and adoring the Lamb who allows us to celebrate the Pasch with him, we are taught not to bow down before man-made idols, and we are given the capacity to obey him whom we recognize as the only Lord of the Church and the world in a spirit of fidelity, docility and veneration.

—Vatican Congregation for Divine Worship, twenty-first century

---

11.

Morning Offering

The human race received a priestly vocation from the moment of its creation. In the book of Genesis, we see that God made a lush garden in Eden, and he placed Adam there "to till it and keep it" (Gen 2:15). Those verbs—in Hebrew, *'abodah* and *shamar*—comprise man's primal vocation. Yet, in all the rest of the Old Testament, they appear together only to describe the priestly service of the tribe of Levi (see Nm 3:7–8, 8:26, 18:5–6), who offered sacrifice and guarded Israel's sanctuary from defilement.

The author's intention is clear to those who read the book in Hebrew: the world was created to be a Temple, and Adam to be its priest. His office was to be passed down through the generations, but Adam forfeited that hereditary right when he committed the original sin.

In the early morning of creation, God conferred priesthood along with human nature. We're hardwired for priesthood. We won't be fulfilled unless we exercise it. So it's in our best interest to understand what the Bible means by priesthood.

In the ancient world, sacrifice was essential to religion, and a priest was someone who had the right and duty to offer sacrifice. A priest stood as a mediator between God and man. In the age of the patriarchs, religion was a family matter, and priesthood was passed down from the father to his firstborn son. When God called the tribes of Israel out of Egypt, he declared that they should be "a kingdom of priests and a holy nation" (Ex 19:6). Yet Israel, like Adam, forfeited the office when the people sinned by worshipping the golden calf. Afterward, priesthood was reserved for the tribe of Levi, whose members had refused to take part in the idolatry.

In the time of Jesus, the Levites offered sacrifice in the Jerusalem Temple. They operated around the clock in swing shifts, offering sacrifices of slaughtered animals, grain, wine, and incense. Supremely important, however, was the first offering of the day. Once the priests had discerned the first glimmer of dawn, they would begin the morning sacrifice. It was a whole burnt offering of a yearling lamb, given to God while the priests renewed the incense offerings as well. Only a perfect, unblemished lamb would do; and so the priests inspected the animal thoroughly, not once, but twice. The lamb's blood was caught up in vessels made of precious metals and reserved only for that purpose. Then the gates of the Temple were opened, to the sound of a blast from silver trumpets.

In all of this morning ritual, the priests of Jerusalem strove, symbolically, to be faithful where Adam had failed and where Israel had failed in the desert. They offered the day to God by offering him a life in its entirety, a life whose purity was scrupulously guarded.

The New Testament clearly presents Jesus as a New Adam

(1 Cor 15:45), a new high priest (see Heb 2–9), an unblemished lamb (Jn 19:36; 1 Cor 5:7). St. Paul spoke of Jesus as both sacrificial priest and sacrificial victim (see Eph 5:2).

Yet Jesus does not exercise his priesthood alone. He has restored it to the human race through the Catholic Church. He has "made us a kingdom, priests to his God and Father" (Rev 1:6; see also Rev 5:10). He has made us "a chosen race, a royal priesthood" (1 Pt 2:9).

We are called to make an offering of our life, as Jesus did, succeeding where Adam had failed and fulfilling the role the Temple priests had prefigured symbolically. We share in Christ's priesthood because, through baptism, we share in his life, not only his divine nature (2 Pt 1:4), but also his human nature, which is restored in its integrity. In him we can fulfill that primal, priestly vocation that is both sacred and secular. We can sanctify the temporal order and offer it to God, restoring it "in Christ" because we live in Christ. We restore it, a little bit at a time, beginning with the inch or the yard or the acre over which we've been given dominion. Our work space, our living space—these are where we exercise our kingship and our priesthood. Our altar is our desktop, our workstation, the row that we hoe, the ditch that we dig, the diaper we change, the pot that we stir, the bed that we share with our spouse. "Everything belongs to you," said St. Paul, ". . . and you to Christ, and Christ to God" (1 Cor 3:22–23).

One way that Catholics exercise this priestly vocation is by praying a "Morning Offering" every day, as soon as they rise from sleep.

In the time of Jesus, there was a prayer that pious Jews prayed every morning. Jews still pray it today. Jesus knew it by heart, and he assumed that all his listeners were familiar with it.

> Hear, O Israel: The Lord our God, the Lord is one; and you shall love the Lord your God with all your heart, and with all your soul, and with all your mind, and with all your strength. (Mk 12:29–30; see also Dt 6:4–5)

The Temple priests prayed these words as they offered the morning sacrifice. Yet all Jews, everywhere on earth, were to recite them as well. It was their virtual participation in the sacrifice of the Temple. It was an explicit offering of the things that Adam had held back: his *whole* heart, his *whole* soul, his *whole* mind, and *all* his strength.

Since the mid-nineteenth century, the Church has urged its members to make a similar priestly offering every day, in union with the holy sacrifice of the Mass. The Morning Offering prayer was first actively promoted by members of the Society of Jesus, the Jesuits. Eventually, the prayer became the cornerstone of the spirituality of an institution called the Apostleship of Prayer, established to encourage the faithful to pray for the pope's intentions, announced monthly.

In 2005 the Synod of Bishops spoke of this as a "eucharistic spirituality and sanctification of the world." Thus, in Christ the New Adam, the priestly people offer a *renewed* creation to God. The cosmos has once again become a sanctuary, with mankind as its nation of priests. "The meaning of all Christian life is union with Christ, who offers himself to the Father for the life of humanity. This is the 'eucharistic form.' This is the beauty of the daily offering taught by the Apostolate of Prayer, which invites the faithful to assume 'eucharistic form,' uniting their life with Mary to the heart of Christ who offers Himself for humanity."

There are many prayers available that we can use for a Morning Offering. We may even make up our own. The text promoted by the Apostleship has developed over the last century and a half. It is brief, but theologically rich:

> O Jesus, through the Immaculate Heart of Mary, I offer you my prayers, works, joys and sufferings of this day for all the intentions of your Sacred Heart, in union with the Holy Sacrifice of the Mass throughout the world, in reparation for my sins, for the intentions of all my relatives and friends, and in particular for the intentions of the Holy Father.

Our day need not begin laboriously, as did the days in the Temple. We need no special bowls or trumpets for our priesthood. Our lamb has already been sacrificed. Now, in the fullness of time, we, with a simple prayer, begin to restore all things in Christ (see Eph 1:10).

Ponder in Your Heart

> The supreme and eternal Priest, Christ Jesus, since he wills to continue his witness and service also through the laity, vivifies them in this Spirit and increasingly urges them on to every good and perfect work.
>
> For besides intimately linking them to his life and his mission, he also gives them a sharing in his priestly function of offering spiritual worship for the glory of God and the salvation of men. For this reason the laity, dedicated to Christ and anointed by the Holy Spirit, are marvelously called and wonderfully prepared so that ever more abundant fruits of the Spirit may be produced in them. For all their works, prayers and apostolic endeavors, their ordinary married and family

life, their daily occupations, their physical and mental relaxation, if carried out in the Spirit, and even the hardships of life, if patiently borne—all these become "spiritual sacrifices acceptable to God through Jesus Christ." Together with the offering of the Lord's body, they are most fittingly offered in the celebration of the Eucharist. Thus, as those everywhere who adore in holy activity, the laity consecrate the world itself to God.

—Second Vatican Council, twentieth century

12.

Prayers of Aspiration

Amid rigorous bodily fasting, the monks and hermits of the desert, in the early centuries of Christianity, would feed their souls upon the Word of God. In some places they would pray all the Psalms every day. Certain lines would seem to express the monk's own thoughts—his fears, joys, frustrations, or desires—and so he would store these away in his mind, to be retrieved for prayer during his manual labor later in the day.

If we live in the workaday world, we don't have the time to pray every Psalm every day. Nor can we work attentively while fasting the way the Desert Fathers did. We can, however, learn much from the way their scriptural recitation led to abundant prayer. In fact, Pope John Paul II proposed their method to the entire Church, encouraging us to store up "concise phrases from the Psalms" that we can "let fly almost like flaming arrows, for example, against temptations."

That's helpful, because we, like those ancient monks, face the enormous challenge Jesus placed before us: to "pray without ceasing and not lose heart" (Lk 18:1). St. Paul echoed it with his exhortation to "pray always" (1 Thes 5:16).

It seems like an unreasonable demand, an impossible requirement, but it's not. For neither Jesus nor St. Paul meant that we should *say prayers* without ceasing. They intended for us to make our lives into prayer—all our prayers, works, joys, and sufferings—as we do virtually in the Morning Offering. It's good for us to renew that offering periodically through the day. In our relationship with God, we want to be like young sweethearts, who think of one another not only when they're together or writing messages or talking on the phone. Their love is constant, and it comes to mind often in the midst of the day's otherwise consuming tasks. I speak from experience when I say that a husband thinks often of his wife in the course of an eight-hour shift away from home, and he thinks in terms of gratitude, admiration, wonder—and, yes, sometimes bafflement. All of those may be appropriately applied to our relationship with God as well.

As people of prayer, we need to take a lesson from young lovers. St. Augustine put it well, around A.D. 412, in a letter to a young widow, the mother of a large family. She wanted to know when she would ever have time for prayer. He assured her that "to spend a long time in prayer is not, as some people think, the same thing as to pray with much speaking. Multiplied words are one thing; long-continued warmth of desire is another."

To shift the metaphor a little bit: if prayer is like a fire, then prayers of aspiration are like logs we place in the flames during the day. St. Augustine adapted the methods of the Desert Fathers for the widow Proba: "The brethren in Egypt are reported to have very frequent prayers, but these very brief, and, as it were, sudden . . . For in most cases prayer consists more in groaning than in speaking, in tears rather than in words. But [God] sets our tears in his sight, and our groaning is not hidden from him who made all things by the word, and does not need human words."

Prayers of aspiration are the ideal prayers to fill otherwise idle moments in our day: long stops at traffic lights, long periods "on hold" as we wait for a call to go through, long hours of insomnia, long delays in a waiting room. We can look at these moments as opportunities or nuisances. We can allow them to fuel our aggravation or fuel our prayer. The choice is ours. And we do have to choose—because nature abhors a vacuum. If we do not fill our mind with prayer, it will fill itself with anxieties, worries, temptations, resentments, and unwelcome memories.

The early Christians used brief aspirations in prayer, and the evidence is all over the New Testament. One of my favorites is the Aramaic *maranatha,* which means, "Come, Lord!" St. Paul prays it (1 Cor 16:22). The same phrase appears in the first-century manual of church order, the *Didache.*

For subsequent generations, the New Testament itself served as a treasure chest of aspirations.

"Lord, you know all things. You know that I love you" (Jn 21:17).
"Not as I will, but as you will" (Mt 26:39).
"I believe; help my unbelief!" (Mk 9:24).
"Jesus, Son of David, have pity on me" (Mk 10:47).
"With God all things are possible" (Mt 19:26).
"He must increase; I must decrease" (Jn 3:30).

The characters in the Gospels—whether blind beggars or chastened apostles—often want to express extremes of emotion in very few words, because Christ was passing by. They teach us how to get to the point, and they even give us pointed words to keep as arrows in our quiver.

Then there are the Psalms, which—as the Desert Fathers knew—offer the range of feelings that humans might want to express in prayer:

"O God, come to my assistance! Lord, make haste to help me!" (Ps 70:1).
"Teach me your ways, O Lord" (Ps 25:4).
"Create in me a clean heart, O God" (Ps 51:10).
"Praise the Lord . . . who heals the brokenhearted" (Ps 147:1, 3).
"My soul thirsts for you" (Ps 63:1).

The liturgy, too, gives us profound phrases we can use to offer adoration, praise, contrition, or supplication. St. Francis de Sales recommended that we pray our favorite lines from hymns. These have the added advantage of melody, which keeps them in our minds and on our lips.

Yet St. Francis also warned us not to limit ourselves to the exact words of formal prayers. We are free to make them our own, and we should. We can also make up our own aspirations from scratch: "speak with heart or mouth whatever springs forth from the love within you, which is sure to supply you with all abundance."

We can even take our cues from nature, as the saints did, for the earth indeed proclaims God's goodness. We should cultivate the habit of referring the things we see, feel, and hear to God their creator: the song of birds, the rush of the wind, the fall of raindrops, the warmth of the midday sun. The fourth-century poet-bishop St. Gregory Nazianzen said he wanted to turn all the things of the world to his own spiritual profit. Now, if there's one way we should want to exploit natural resources, that's it!

Ponder in Your Heart

Aspire continually to God, by brief, ardent upliftings of the heart; praise his excellence, invoke his aid, cast yourself in spirit at the foot of his cross, adore his goodness, offer your whole soul a thousand times a day to him, fix your inward gaze upon him, stretch out your hands to be led by him, as a little child to its father, clasp him to your breast as a fragrant flower, raise him up in your soul as a standard. In short, kindle by every possible act your love for God, your tender, passionate desire for the heavenly Bridegroom of souls . . . Neither is this a difficult practice—it may be interwoven with all our duties and occupations, without hindering any; for neither the spiritual retreat of which I have spoken, nor these inward upliftings of the heart, cause more than a very brief distraction, which, so far from being any hindrance, will rather promote whatever you have in hand . . .

Just as those who are full of some earthly, natural love are ever turning in thought to the beloved one, their hearts overflowing with tenderness, and their lips ever ready to praise that beloved object; comforting themselves in absence by letters, carving the treasured name on every tree—so those who love God cannot cease thinking of him, living for him, longing after him, speaking of him . . . And to such an outpouring of love all creation bids us—everything he has made is filled with the praise of God, and, as says St. Augustine, everything in the world speaks silently but clearly to the lovers of God of their love, exciting them to holy desires, whence gush forth aspirations and loving cries to God.

—St. Francis de Sales, seventeenth century

13.

The Angelus

Moses lived a long life, full of dramatic moments. One of the most justly famous, however, is the story of his role in Israel's great battle with Amalek. Already quite elderly, Moses watched the battle from a hill nearby. "Whenever Moses held up his hand"—in a gesture of humble prayer—"Israel prevailed; and whenever he lowered his hand, Amalek prevailed" (Ex 17:11). Midway through the battle, Moses' arms grew weary and began to fall. So his brother Aaron and friend Hur flanked him and supported his hands, so that they were steady until the end of the battle. Israel was, of course, victorious.

We who do not possess Moses' greatness can also grow weary midway through our daily struggles. So we pause at midday to renew our flagging efforts in prayer. The traditional Catholic midday prayer is called the Angelus. It is a prayer for two or more voices—verses with responses, each followed by a recitation of the "Hail Mary"—but it may be prayed alone.

The verses and responses are scriptural, drawn from the story of Jesus' conception, as told in the Gospels of Luke (1:26–28 and 1:38) and John (1:14). Thus, at the turning point of our day, we remember the turning point of human history: the moment when an angel appeared to a young woman named Mary and told her of God's plan to send the Messiah to the world as her child. All subsequent history, and all of creation, turned on her consent.

Angelus is Latin for "angel," which is the first word of the prayer in Latin. Here is a common English translation:

V. The Angel of the Lord declared unto Mary.
R. And she conceived by the Holy Spirit.
Hail Mary, full of grace . . .
V. Behold the handmaid of the Lord.
R. Be it done unto me according to thy word.
Hail Mary, full of grace . . .
V. And the Word was made Flesh.
R. And dwelt among us.
Hail Mary, full of grace . . .
V. Pray for us, O holy Mother of God.
R. That we may be made worthy of the promises of Christ.

Let us pray: Pour forth we beseech thee, O Lord, thy grace into our hearts, that we, to whom the incarnation of Christ thy Son was made known by the message of an angel, may by his passion and cross be brought to the glory of his resurrection. Through the same Christ Our Lord. Amen.

Though Catholics most commonly recite the Angelus at noon, some pray it also at six in the morning and six in the evening.

That's why churches ring the "angelus bells" at those hours. (In the Middle Ages, it was, for this reason, customary to inscribe the name of the angel Gabriel on church bells.)

During the fifty days from Easter Sunday to Pentecost Sunday, we replace the Angelus prayer with the Regina Caeli ("Queen of Heaven"), recited at the same time (or times).

V. Queen of Heaven, rejoice, alleluia.
R. For He whom you did merit to bear, alleluia.
V. Has risen, as he said, alleluia.
R. Pray for us to God, alleluia.
V. Rejoice and be glad, O Virgin Mary, alleluia.
R. For the Lord has truly risen, alleluia.

Let us pray: O God, who gave joy to the world through the resurrection of thy Son, our Lord Jesus Christ, grant we beseech thee, that through the intercession of the Virgin Mary, his mother, we may obtain the joys of everlasting life. Through the same Christ our Lord. Amen.

Christians have always paused for prayer at the noon hour. In apostolic times, it was called the prayer of the "sixth hour," counting from sunrise. St. Peter was praying the noontime prayers when he received a revelation from the Lord (Acts 10:9).

It was also at the sixth hour that Jesus was crucified (Lk 23:44), his arms outstretched as Moses' arms were, on yet another hilltop. In prayer he persevered and prevailed, even over death.

The early Christians remembered these biblical events and precedents as they offered their customary midday prayers, which Tertullian recorded as early as the second century.

If we are growing weak or weary at midday, or irritable with our coworkers or family, if we are discouraged because the odds are against us, we can look to Mary and know that we, too, can rely on the help of angels and the providence of God, who has a plan for us. Like Moses, we can renew our prayer, with supernatural help, and witness the victory of God in our hearts through the rest of the day.

Ponder in Your Heart

What we have to say about the Angelus is meant to be only a simple but earnest exhortation to continue its traditional recitation wherever and whenever possible. The Angelus does not need to be revised, because of its simple structure, its biblical character, its historical origin which links it to the prayer for peace and safety, and its quasi-liturgical rhythm which sanctifies different moments during the day, and because it reminds us of the Paschal Mystery, in which recalling the incarnation of the Son of God we pray that we may be led "through his passion and cross to the glory of his resurrection." These factors ensure that the Angelus despite the passing of centuries retains an unaltered value and an intact freshness. It is true that certain customs traditionally linked with the recitation of the Angelus have disappeared or can continue only with difficulty in modern life. But these are marginal elements. The value of contemplation on the mystery of the incarnation of the Word, of the greeting to the Virgin, and of recourse to her merciful intercession remains unchanged. And despite the changed conditions of the times, for the majority of people there remain unaltered the characteristic periods of the day—morning, noon and evening—which mark the periods of their activity and constitute an invitation to pause in prayer.

—Pope Paul VI, twentieth century

14.

Grace at Meals

Back in chapter 1, we spoke of water as a "sacrament" in all the ages of creation. In the age of nature it was a "natural sacrament"—a sign of something greater still to come. In the age of grace, it is a supernatural sacrament: baptism, which gives us supernatural life. In the age of glory, the signs will give way to the signified, and we will know heaven's "river of the water of life" (Rev 22:1), which is the grace of the Holy Spirit.

What applies to water applies also to our "daily bread." St. Thomas Aquinas noted that bread, like water, has always provided sustenance for man in the order of nature; yet, in its "natural" state, it also prefigured the unleavened bread of the Passover and the manna that rained down in the desert. All of these in turn foreshadowed the Holy Eucharist, which Jesus established in the age of grace. St. Thomas explains: "each is a symbol of the spiritual food. But they are different because [the manna] was only a symbol," while the Eucharist of the Christians contains what it symbolizes, "that is, Christ himself."

In ancient Israel, bread was what made a meal a meal. A meal was incomplete without bread. Indeed, for most families, bread made up the most substantial portion of every meal. Meat was a luxury. So the customary prayers at mealtime—what we have come to call "grace at meals"—were, in those days, called "blessing over bread." It was the blessing that transformed a natural occurrence—that is, feeding—into a sacred event.

The ancient Jewish table blessing will resonate with Catholics, as it has had a profound influence on the prayers of the Mass. The earliest Christian liturgies—the Syriac Liturgy of Addai and Mari and the Egyptian Liturgy of St. Mark—include the text, more or less intact.

Blessed are you, Lord, God, King of the universe. You nourish the whole world with goodness, tender love, and mercy. Blessed are you, Lord, who nourish the universe. We will give you thanks, Lord our God . . .

Every meal, then, was a celebration of God's creation and his providence. By means of the common prayers, every meal was united with the historic meals of the ancestors: the hospitality of Abraham toward his three heavenly visitors (Gen 18:1–8), the king's table on Mount Zion (2 Sam 9:12), Wisdom's banquet of bread and wine (Prv 9:1–5), the feast of fulfillment in the prophet Isaiah: "On this mountain the Lord of hosts will make for all peoples a feast of fat things, a feast of wine on the lees, of fat things full of marrow, of wine on the lees well refined . . . You shall have a song as in the night when a holy feast is kept" (Is 25:6, 30:29).

The invocation of the Lord was also an evocation of the Temple, where the perpetual sacrifices were seen as "meals eaten in the presence of God."

The New Testament shows us Jesus as he vividly brings all these meals to fulfillment. Commentators note that the drama of St.

Luke's Gospel unfolds over the course of ten meal scenes, culminating in the Last Supper and the Eucharist at Emmaus. We have already seen how this New Covenant meal established communion, *chaburah,* not only among God's people, but also between God and man. Now, it is more than a meal taken in God's *presence.* It is a meal shared with God himself—and with God himself as the substance of the meal.

This is, in the age of grace, the image of the banquet the saints know in heaven. When we "say grace" before (or after) our meals, we transform our homey family meals—and even our meals taken alone—into "sacraments" of God's banquet.

The prayer lends every meal an importance and dignity it might otherwise lack. Perhaps this is why the apostles, who were Jews, had trouble getting pagan converts to understand the solemnity of sacred meals (see 1 Cor 11; Jude 12).

This doesn't mean our family meals or meals with friends will be stiff or joyless or unnecessarily formal. If anything, it should increase the joy, because an awareness of God's presence will surely inspire us to love those around us all the more and all the better. (It will probably help us to eat temperately, too.)

The question sometimes arises whether we should say grace in public places, or when eating with a mixed group of Christians and non-Christians. I think it's always a good idea, even if we offer our prayer silently while making an unostentatious Sign of the Cross. This simple gesture sometimes has a profound effect on bystanders, and it has even marked the beginning of conversion for people who have witnessed it. We must not underestimate the power of such simple public witness. Sometimes a quiet gesture speaks louder and more eloquently than a thousand words shouted on a street corner. This is especially true when that gesture is so suggestive of the Eucharist—and every meal, in the Old Testament and the New, that finds fulfillment in the Eucharist. "Grace" can be a mighty conveyor of grace!

It takes no great effort. There are many prayers available for our use, and we can even make up our own. The most common grace before meals runs like this: "Bless us, O Lord, and these, thy gifts, which we are about to receive from thy bounty. Through Christ, our Lord. Amen."

The most common grace after meals is similar: "We give thee thanks, Almighty God, for these and all thy gifts, which we have received from thy bounty. Who lives and reigns world without end. Amen."

Ponder in Your Heart

O Lord our God, you are the Bread that is eaten in heaven, the Bread that gives life, the Food that really nourishes the whole world. You came down from heaven and gave the world life; you guide us through this present existence, and you have promised that there will be another for us to enjoy after this. Bless, then, our food and drink and enable us to take them without sinning. May we receive them thankfully and give you glory for them, for you it is who confer all good gifts upon us. Blessed and glorious is your name, ever worthy of honor.

—Anonymous, Ancient Greek Prayerbook

15.

EXAMINATION OF CONSCIENCE

If you keep a budget at home, you know one fact about accounting. It's something you have to do regularly. You have to watch what you're spending on groceries, on entertainment, on utilities. If your heating bill is your undoing, you have to keep your eye on the thermostat every day, not just in the last week of the month. Businesses do the same. Accounting is their way of life, and their world turns on receipts, ledgers, expense reports, and planned depreciation.

In the business of salvation, too, there's an accounting we have to do. In the book of Revelation, St. John evokes a ledger book when he speaks of the Book of Life. Well, unless we do some daily accounting, we're not going to make daily or monthly improvement, and we'll be unlikely to show a profit when we face that final audit.

Our daily spiritual "accounting" is called the examination of conscience. It's the time we take to review the day's events and our own thoughts, words, and deeds. We try to see the day as God sees it, and judge our actions as he would. It's a chance to be perfectly honest with ourselves about who we are, what we do, and why we do it. The exam makes us aware of our progress, or regress, and keeps us focused on what's real.

Spiritual writers usually divide the examination into two parts: *general* and *particular.* The general exam is an overall review of the day—what we did, thought, felt, said, or failed to do. In the particular exam, we measure how we're doing in a specific struggle—resisting a certain sin or acquiring a certain virtue. St. Josemaría Escrivá said it well: "The general examination is a weapon of defense. The particular, of attack. The first is the shield. The second, the sword." Most people make their general exam near bedtime, so that it's complete. Some people make their particular exam at noon (with the Angelus), so that they can resolve to redouble efforts for the remainder of the day.

The best way to begin is to recollect ourselves in God's presence, to remind ourselves that he's with us, and then to start the conversation. If we do this, we'll find it pretty hard to be dishonest in our examination. After all, who are we fooling? Surely not God, who knows all and sees all.

Then we should ask God for light, and try to see our day as he sees it—not as we wish it had gone, but as we lived it in our heart. We can do this as a chronological look at the day, from waking till right now. Or we can consider each of the Ten Commandments and how well we lived them. Some prayer books contain questions for self-examination, and these can be very helpful. Or we can compile our own list of questions, based on advice we get from our spouse, friends, or spiritual director.

Three minutes is plenty of time to consider the whole day. We should concentrate on all our actions of the day, not just the big ones. If we excuse ourselves on "little things"—"little" white lies, "little" incidents of gluttony, momentary but deliberate glances at billboard nudity—we'll never get around to doing big things (or even medium-sized things) for God. We'll be stuck in sin and mediocrity.

At the end of our time, we should tell God we're sorry and ask forgiveness with an act of contrition. It could be the one you learned in grade school, or just a short aspiration like "Lord Jesus Christ, Son of God, have mercy on me, a sinner." Then make resolutions for the next day. You might even write them down, so you don't lose them in your sleep.

As we grow in this practice, we'll see patterns develop. We shouldn't be discouraged if we find ourselves facing up to the same sins day after day. Seeing a pattern is actually a sign of progress. Our disgust at the sin is yet another sign of progress. It all depends on what we do with it.

One thing not to do is give up. Stick with the exam and talk to our Lord about it. Ask him for help. Gaining a virtue or losing a habit of sin might take years, but we will win, with God's help.

When we've homed in on one virtue to acquire, or a vice we need to lose, then we have material for our particular exam. It's best to be very specific here and set steady, achievable goals. Some people are given to pessimism, bad attitude, and despair. They might take a hard look at how well they live the virtue of hope. When they voice their opinions on world events, or everyday business matters, or the economy, do they sound like dark disciples of gloom and doom? Or like children of God, who know that their world is in their good Father's hands?

Other people will need to concentrate on other sins: pride and boasting, lust, lying, jealousy. Or perhaps more positively, the corresponding virtues: humility and service, purity, honesty, magnanimity.

The particular exam is a good place to use advice from our spiritual director. He can help us focus our attention on the fault that needs our attention right now. We don't want to waste our time dusting shelves when the roof is about to collapse. A good spiritual director will point us to the falling roof—the sin that, perhaps, we've been avoiding even in our prayer.

St. Thomas Aquinas said that honest memory is the first prerequisite for all the other virtues. For that reason, we shouldn't underestimate the importance of the examination of conscience. In our fallen nature, we have a tendency to deceive ourselves. We want to believe good things about ourselves, our actions, and our motivations. We try to cover up the unpleasant things we've thought and said and done—we make excuses for them, or explain them away. The grave danger, though, is that we eventually begin to believe ourselves. Such falsification of memory is one of our deadliest enemies. It covers up the signposts on roads that lead to hell.

When we've been at it for a while, we find that the exam becomes more than an event in our day. It becomes a habit, part of our life from hour to hour, action to action. We come to see more clearly that all our life, in thought and deed, is lived in God's sight. So we can see a course of action immediately as right or wrong. We become used to referring our conversations, our work, our choices to our Lord.

St. Paul insisted (1 Cor 11:28–31) that "a man should examine himself" before receiving Holy Communion, and he warned that laxity in self-examination was leading people to receive Jesus unworthily: "That is why many among you are sick and infirm, and why so many are dying." We don't want such things to happen to us.

If we're regularly examining our conscience, we'll find it natural to go regularly to confession. We'll go ready to tell our sins to God and receive his assurance of forgiveness. Because confession is a sacrament, it confers an abundance of grace on us. Grace is the strength we need to conquer sins, in general and in particular.

Ponder in Your Heart

1. In the morning, as soon as you wake up, make up your mind to watch most carefully lest you fall into that particular defect which you wish to correct.
2. During the day, when you notice that you have erred, at once with some interior prayer . . . ask God for His forgiveness; with your hand on your heart, promise to be more attentive in the future.
3. In the evening when you make your general examination, after having made a general survey of all your faults, give particular attention to this one.
4. Compare the second day with the first, the third with the second . . . and so on. In this way, you will know whether or not you are progressing in virtue, and whether you are getting any good out of the particular examination.
5. You may also make some virtue the subject of the particular examination. Those who make the particular and general examination in the evening when they go to bed, as well as during the day, redouble their speed and in a short time make further progress along the road of virtue.

—Angelo Roncalli (later Pope John XXIII), twentieth century

IV

Life Lessons

16.

Bible Study

As Catholics, we believe that the Bible is the written Word of God. It is "inspired by God" (2 Tim 3:16). It is not a dead letter, but "living and active" (Heb 4:12). It "must be fulfilled" (Lk 22:37) and "cannot be broken" (Jn 10:35). What's more, it is not subject merely to private interpretation (2 Pt 1:20), but to the discernment of the Church, because people can easily "twist" Scripture "to their own destruction" (2 Pt 3:16).

The Bible is as sharp as any two-edged sword (Heb 4:12), and thus it should be handled with care. *Yet it should indeed be handled.* The Bible itself exhorts us to attend to Bible study (1 Tim 4:13) and praises those who "examine the Scriptures daily" (Acts 17:11).

We live in a time of unprecedented opportunities for Bible study. Never before have so many people on earth had such instant access to the Scriptures. Remember, for most of Christian history, the majority of people could not read; and many of those who *could* read could not afford to own books. In the centuries before the invention of the printing press (in the fifteenth century), books had to be copied out, laboriously and expensively, by hand.

Today, however, even most *poor* Christians have opportunities to own their own Bible. Publishers print editions small enough to fit in a purse or pocket and go with us wherever we go. So any unplanned downtime can become time for Scripture study.

When we're puzzled, we can summon help—again, as never before. Online Bibles enable us to search the Scriptures with speed and accuracy that the ancients thought impossible this side of heaven. We are capable of conducting research, in seconds, that the Church Fathers could not have accomplished in a lifetime.

Yet even with all these advances, studies seem to indicate that biblical literacy is declining—and there is little difference in Bible-reading habits between Catholics and Protestants.

Why is biblical literacy in such seemingly universal decline? I believe it's because Christians have lost the habit of "reading the Bible from the heart of the Church."

That phrase can have many meanings, all of them true. It suggests the dispositions we should have when we approach the Scriptures: we are trusting children of God and of the Church, our mother. We read the sacred page within a community that's much larger than any local Bible-study group. Our "study group" is the Communion of Saints, the voices of Catholic tradition, the great cloud of witnesses from all of history. Our guide is the Holy Spirit, working through the Church's bishops and pope.

Most importantly, we should read the Bible in its natural and supernatural habitat. We should read the Bible in light of the liturgy.

The Bible and the liturgy were made for one another. That statement would have seemed self-evident to the apostles and the

Church Fathers. There were no printing presses in their day, and very few people could afford to have books copied out by hand. So people did not so much read the Scriptures as absorb them, mostly in the Mass. The Mass itself is a stunning compendium of scriptural texts, and it has always included extended readings from both testaments.

In the early Church, the Bible was considered a liturgical book. Indeed, the canon—the official "list" of books in the Bible—was originally drawn up to limit the texts that could be used as readings in the Mass.

Yet the connection goes back even further than that. For the scriptural texts themselves presume the context of the Mass. The apostles and evangelists seem to be writing with liturgical proclamation in mind.

If we read the Bible as they wrote it, we'll read it from the heart of the Church, and that heart is eucharistic. It is the heart of Jesus.

In the 1970s the Catholic Church revised its lectionary—the order of scriptural readings for the Mass. The readings now unfold in a three-year cycle and include almost all the books of both testaments of the Bible. The schema proved so effective in communicating the Word of God that it has been adopted and adapted by many Protestant bodies as well.

The great thing about the lectionary is that it not only presents the Scriptures, but it also teaches us a method of understanding the Scriptures. Every week—almost every day—the readings present revelation's movement from Old Covenant to New, a consistent pattern of promise and fulfillment. The New Testament is concealed in the Old, and the Old is revealed in the New.

This is why I'm optimistic about Catholic Bible study—because the Mass enables us to build up from a strong foundation, according to time-tested methods.

What's more, so many Catholics are at least intermittently exposed to the program. The Mass is the one thing that Catholics are supposed to experience on a weekly basis all their lives; and the Bible is the one book that they will hear at every Mass. Since Masses on Sundays and holy days usually include three readings from the two testaments, plus a fourth from the book of Psalms, the average faithful Catholic spends about fifteen hours a year in focused Bible study. If you include the other overtly biblical parts of the Mass (the "Holy, Holy, Holy," the "Lamb of God," the "Lord, Have Mercy," and so on), the average time per annum doubles or triples. For the Catholic who goes to daily Mass, the totals are quite impressive, rivaling even the hours spent by some scholars.

Scholars have written mighty tomes, and saints have spent long lives, teaching people what it means to read the Bible faithfully. Here I'll offer just a brief word on interpretation—three short principles that were decreed by the Second Vatican Council and summarized in the *Catechism of the Catholic Church:*

1. "Be attentive 'to the content and unity of the whole Scripture' " (n. 112).
2. "Read the Scripture within 'the living Tradition of the whole Church' " (n. 113).
3. "Be attentive to the analogy of faith" (n. 114).

The Church's first criterion protects us from wrenching verses out of context, making them out to mean something other than their divine and human authors intended. The true context of every verse in the Bible is the book in which it appears—not only the book of the Bible, but also the book that *is* the Bible. The complete literary context of any Scripture verse includes all the books from Genesis to Revelation, because the Bible is a unified book, not merely a library of different books.

The second criterion places the Bible firmly within the context of a community that treasures a "living tradition." That community is the Communion of Saints. We test our own interpretations, measuring them against the tradition of interpreters who have gone before us. G. K. Chesterton called this principle the "democracy of the dead." We believe that our ancestors have much to teach us. They should have a vote. It protects us from the ever-present arrogance of believing we have just now reached the pinnacle of human knowledge and insight. Catholics should have the humility to learn from the past, and to know that the tradition is still *living* today, in the preaching of the saints and the teachings of the Church. Scholarly fads will come and go. The truth abides, unchanging.

The third criterion leads us to examine scriptural texts within the framework of the fullness of Catholic faith. If we believe that the Scriptures are divinely inspired, we must also believe them to be internally coherent and consistent with all Catholic doctrine. The Church's dogmas are not something added to Scripture. In the words of Cardinal Joseph Ratzinger (later Pope Benedict XVI): "Dogma is by definition nothing other than an interpretation of Scripture." Dogmas are the Church's *infallible* interpretation of Scripture.

No one should be better prepared for Bible study than a faithful Catholic. It doesn't require a doctorate—though God bless those faithful Catholics who decide to pursue their studies so far, and may their tribe increase! Many saints down the centuries, however, had to content themselves with opportunities much humbler than you and I have today. In the Church, we have all we need for understanding the Scriptures—and making our own way to sainthood.

Ponder in Your Heart

I remember our Latvian priest, Viktors, who during the Soviet regime in Latvia was arrested for possessing the Holy Bible. In the eyes of the Soviet agents the Holy Scriptures were an anti-revolutionary book. The agents threw the Holy Scriptures on the floor and ordered the priest to step on it. The priest refused and instead knelt down and kissed the book. For this gesture the priest was condemned to ten years of hard labor in Siberia. Ten years later when the priest returned to his parish and celebrated the Holy Mass, he read the Gospel. Then he lifted up the lectionary and said: "The Word of God!" The people cried and thanked God. They did not dare to applaud him, because that would be understood as another provocation.

In Latvia during the Soviet era no religious books, no Holy Scriptures, no catechisms were allowed to be printed. The reasoning was, if there is no printed Word of God, there will be no religion. Our Latvian people did what the first-century Christians did: they learnt the passages of the Holy Scriptures by heart. Still today in Latvia there is an oral tradition alive. We stand on the shoulders of our martyrs to proclaim the Word of God. Our grandchildren remember their grandfathers and grandmothers, who died for their faith, and they want to be, in their turn, the heroes of faith.

In Latvia we proclaim the living Word of God! We go in the processions and on the pilgrimages, we sing songs and we pray and say: "This is the Word of God," for which our grandparents died. In Latvia when the Holy Mass is only one hour long, the people say it's only a warm-up for the real encounter with God in Sacrament and His Word.

—Bishop Antons Justs, twenty-first century

17.

SPIRITUAL READING

One of the leading lights of the fourth century, St. Epiphanius, said: "The acquisition of Christian books is necessary for those who can use them. For the mere sight of these books renders us less inclined to sin, and incites us to believe more firmly in righteousness."

In my world, he's what is known as an enabler. I'm fairly addicted to books, so there's hardly a spot in my home where I'm left vulnerable to sin. Christian books are always in sight.

I recognize that not everyone is as avid a reader as I am (though if you've read this far, you're obviously no slouch yourself). But even I am sometimes less inclined to read the things I *need* to read—books and articles for work, or for household business, or books assigned by higher authorities, like my dean, my confessor, or my wife. So I have to remind myself every now and then that *reading requires discipline.*

Spiritual reading, especially, *is* a discipline.

Spiritual reading differs from other reading because it's study we take on, perhaps at the request of a spiritual director, to guide our growth in virtue, knowledge of doctrine, and union with God. It's not reading for entertainment, really, or even for education. It should lead to prayer, and it is itself a form of prayer. A Carthusian abbot named Guigo II summed it up in a now-classic phrase: "Seek in reading and you will find in meditating; knock in mental prayer and it will be opened to you by contemplation." That formula involves a lot of prayer, but prayer that rises upward from a foundation of good, solid reading. Indeed, Guigo warns us that our prayer will suffer if we waste our reading on worthless material.

So what's worthwhile for spiritual reading? It used to be a commonplace that the best authors were those whose names begin with *s*—like St. Augustine, St. Thomas, St. Bonaventure, St. Ignatius, St. Alphonsus, and so on. That still holds true today. When the Church canonizes someone as a saint, the decree is infallible, and so we know that that person is in heaven. Since heaven is our goal, too, the saints map out a path that is proven and trustworthy.

Yet the saints do differ from one another in temperament, methods, and style. So it's very difficult for us to cobble together a spirituality based on scraps from their many and varied spiritualities. We need help finding works that suit us in our particular circumstances. For example: a book that deals with the nitty-gritty of daily life in a monastery might serve as an endless source of wisdom for monks, but still be worse than useless for a family of Catholic laypeople.

Thus, the best works *for you and me* will be those that are assigned to us by an experienced spiritual director or confessor. Indeed, I know a few such men who have published helpful lists that could keep us going for a lifetime. Even so, the personal attention of a spiritual director is irreplaceable. We want to make sure that our spiritual reading does not proceed according to our whims, interests, or idiosyncracies of taste. We might have no inclination to read a book about Trinitarian theology, for instance, or about growth in kindness. Yet these might be precisely the books we need to read—and sooner rather than later. Our spiritual director will know.

Receiving the assignment isn't the end of the "discipline" part. It's good for us to go about our reading, too, in a measured way.

It's not good to consume spiritual books in a gluttonous way, gorging on large portions at a single sitting. It's better for us to treat today's reading like a meal. We should take the words in slowly, for assimilation. We should read a little, pray, and give ourselves a chance to digest what we've taken in. It's okay if we spend as much time in our pauses for reflection as we spend in active reading.

But I'm getting ahead of myself. Our spiritual reading should begin as our meals begin: with a prayer. I favor the Church's standard prayer to the Holy Spirit: "Come, Holy Spirit, fill the hearts of thy faithful and enkindle in them the fire of thy love. Send forth your Spirit and they shall be created, and thou shalt renew the face of the earth." There are many possibilities. One of my favorite spiritual writers, Eugene Boylan, proposed this brief aspiration: "Jesus, give me yourself through this book!"

Father Boylan also emphasized the need for guidance for good reading. He lamented the Catholic laity's aversion to the study of dogma: "Where theology is read by the laity, it is usually rather from the point of view of apologetic argument than from that of a dogmatic foundation for true devotion. We would rather see the reverse." I would, too. Theology can be difficult reading, especially demanding of minds that are untrained in the field. Most Catholics of my generation are untrained even in basic doctrine—never mind theology! Nevertheless, Father Boylan pointed out that "Even if a man's reading of Catholic theology were only enough to teach him to know how much he does not know about it, a lot would be gained."

Our reading should be regular. In fact, it should be daily. It should never be burdensome. We should limit the time we dedicate to the task—say ten or twenty minutes—and keep ourselves within those constraints. It's better for us to devote ten minutes a day to spiritual reading over the course of thirty days than to glut ourselves on five hours in a single day.

If the assigned book doesn't interest us, we should keep reading anyway. Our directors have a "grace of state" to guide us in these matters (see CCC, n. 2004). Remember: we're not reading for esthetic pleasure (though that, too, will come often enough), but rather for nourishment.

Our needs will vary according to our individual circumstances and to the seasons of our lives. So we shouldn't be surprised if we don't always see the sense in our program of reading. Neither should we hesitate to ask permission about books that interest us or seem to suit a current need. The range of books available is indeed vast—christology, lives of the saints, morals, metaphysics, angelology, mariology, catechisms . . . Our directors might even tag a secular book that suits us for spiritual reading.

Father Boylan said that without regular reading "there is no possibility of advancing in the spiritual life: even perseverance therein is rendered very doubtful."

We should all hear the call that St. Augustine heard so long ago: *Tolle, lege! Tolle, lege!* (Take up and read! Take up and read!) It's not a call to be addicted to books. It is a call to a very helpful discipline, and one that's not too much of a burden, at least for some of us.

Ponder in Your Heart

I send you the book on Christian hope that I promised you. It will prove a real treasure to you, but if you wish to derive from it all the fruit that I expect, you must restrain your eagerness to read, and not allow yourself to be carried away by curiosity to know what is coming. Make use of the time allowed by the Rule to read it, concentrate all your attention on what you are actually reading without troubling about the rest. I advise you above all, to enter into the meaning of the consoling and solid truths that you will find laid down in this book; but more in a practical way than by speculative reflections, and, from time to time, make short pauses to allow these truths time to flow through all the recesses of the soul and to give occasion for the operation of the Holy Spirit who, during these peaceful pauses, and times of silent attention, engraves and imprints these heavenly truths in the heart. All this, however, without disturbing your attraction, or violent effort to prevent reflections, but simply and quietly trying to make them enter into your heart more than into your mind.

Take particular notice of certain more important chapters, of which you are in greater need, in order to read them again when next you have time. In general I advise you strongly not to overload your mind with readings and outward practices, it is much better to read little, and to digest what you read. Just now, too, your soul is in need of unity and simplicity, and all your readings and practices should tend to a single end, and that is, to form in you a spirit of recollection.

—Jean-Pierre de Caussade, SJ, eighteenth century

18.

Retreat

Of all the disciplines of prayer preserved in Christian tradition, the Bible speaks at length about only a few. To those passages we should certainly be attentive; to those practices we should certainly be faithful. For there we can be sure to find inspired and inerrant counsel for our spiritual life.

So we can say this with certainty: if we want to advance in the spiritual life, we should first *retreat.*

A "spiritual retreat" is an extended time we take—usually in relative quiet and solitude—to pray and ponder God's will in a sustained and focused way.

Where do we find the practice in Scripture? In many places! Think of Moses, who made a retreat whenever he was about to do something momentous. He left ample time for solitary prayer, and then he went away to be alone with God—and without distractions. "And Moses entered the cloud, and went up on the mountain. And Moses was on the mountain forty days and forty nights" (Ex 24:18).

Moses' retreat was a time of openness toward God. He was preparing to receive the commandments. Yet it was not simply a passive exercise. He took certain disciplines upon himself, to prepare for God's action. He fasted, for example: "And he was there with the Lord forty days and forty nights; he neither ate bread nor drank water" (Ex 34:28).

Nor was Moses the last of the Old Testament saints to make a spiritual retreat. When the prophets wanted to hear the word of the Lord, they sometimes had to withdraw from the noise of workaday life. Elijah retreated to a cave so that he could, eventually, discern God's "still small voice" (1 Kgs 19:12).

The prophets made time for it, because sometimes it takes time to discern God's voice. God called young Samuel several times *by name* before Samuel even recognized who was calling. Only then could Samuel begin to utter the prayer that should be on our own hearts when we make a retreat: "Speak, Lord. Your servant is listening" (1 Sam 3:10).

Jesus' retreats are all the more instructive, as he made them for our benefit. He did not need to make an effort in order to hear God's voice, know the Father's will, or grow in communion with God. Yet he made the effort anyway. "Then Jesus was led up by the Spirit into the wilderness . . . And he fasted forty days and forty nights" (Mt 4:1–2). He also went on retreat when he was, like Moses, about to do something big, like naming his chosen Twelve. Sometimes, too, he went off to grieve in God's presence. It is a deliberate pattern in his life: "he withdrew to the wilderness and prayed" (Lk 5:16) . . . "he withdrew from there in a boat to a lonely place apart" (Mt 14:13) . . . "In these days he went out to the mountain to pray; and all night he continued in prayer to God" (Lk 6:12).

What Jesus said of his actions at the Last Supper applies just as well to those spiritual retreats he made: "I have given you an example, that you also should do as I have done" (Jn 13:15).

The disciples did indeed follow Jesus' lead. In fact, he led them personally on their first retreats. "Jesus took with him Peter and James and John his brother, and led them up a high mountain apart" (Mt 17:1).

So well established was the retreat—time apart in a place apart—that St. Paul did it as a matter of course at the time of his conversion. He spent time fasting (Acts 9:9); he went away into the Arabian desert (Gal 1:17).

At other times, a "retreat" was imposed upon the apostles—in the form of imprisonment or exile. St. John was banished to Patmos when, in prayer, he received the revelations recorded in the Apocalypse (see Rev 1:9).

The fruits of a spiritual retreat were manifold for our scriptural forebearers. From their days spent apart in the wilderness, the prophets and disciples gained spiritual clarity and a strengthened sense of mission. In the cases of Moses and John, their new insights technically qualify as divine revelations!

The fruits of retreat will certainly be manifold for us as well. We should schedule time for a retreat, ideally once a year, and we should be generous with the time. As my children will surely verify: the first characteristic of quality time is quantity. We need ample hours for the kind of conversation God wants us to have with him on retreat. As in a conversation with a beloved friend, we need time in the beginning just to work through the "small talk," just to "catch up" on what's going on in life. We also need time just to detach from our routines and to-do lists. For the first full day of a retreat, I find myself glancing at my watch, instinctively anticipating what comes next in my ordinary workdays. Only after a day of silence am I able to relax in God's presence and truly offer the prayer of young Samuel: "Speak, Lord. Your servant is listening." Only then can I hope to hear that still small voice.

Why do we need the kind of withdrawal that Jesus and St. Paul modeled for us? Because we need to adjust ourselves to a radically different way of thinking. Only then can we begin to discern God's will and honestly judge our lives by his standards. "For my thoughts are not your thoughts nor your ways my ways," says the Lord. "For as the heavens are exalted above the earth, so are my ways exalted above your ways, and my thoughts above your thoughts" (Is 55:8–9). To think like God is a grace, but corresponding to the grace requires some effort on our part, as Jesus showed us. Effort takes time. A retreat gives us time for the effort and a near occasion of grace.

Through its many spiritual families, the Church offers many varieties of retreat experiences: private retreats and group retreats, couples retreats and family retreats, silent retreats and conversational retreats, charismatic retreats and contemplative retreats. They take place in monasteries and convents, campgrounds and hotels, even in special campuses dedicated exclusively to retreats.

I gravitate toward a directed retreat, with lots of time for silent prayer and opportunities, too, for private counsel. I like to leave a retreat having made some judgments on the year behind me, and resolutions for the year ahead. Those judgments and resolutions serve as the most helpful and accurate benchmarks of my spiritual growth.

Only when I make a good retreat am I able to advance with confidence.

Ponder in Your Heart

I made this retreat . . . many times. The first time brought with it a shock of recognition that this was what I was looking for in the way of an explanation of the mystery of the Christian Life, the plan of God for us all. Though still I saw through a glass darkly, I saw things as a whole for the first time with a delight, a joy, an excitement, which is hard to describe. This is what I expected when I became a Catholic. This is what all my reading had led me to expect in the way of teaching and guidance in the spiritual life. I came away with what I can only consider to be an increased knowledge of the supernatural life, the feeling that I had grown in faith, hope and charity, that I had been fed the strong meat of the Gospel and was now prepared to run the race, to journey onward with that food which would sustain me for forty days in any wilderness. I felt prepared for deserts and underground tunnels, for the dark night of the senses and of the soul. And I knew too that this strong light would dim with the ensuing months and that the next year I would again have to make the retreat, to adjust my vision to the blazing truth which was set before us, to get things into perspective once again.

—Dorothy Day, twentieth century

V

Stages of Life

19.

Confirmation

Confirmation has been called a "sacrament in search of a theology," and a canonized saint has referred to the Holy Spirit as "the Great Unknown." Can it be that both our doctrine and our devotion are so impoverished—that we know neither the gift nor the giver?

May it never be so for you and me! For if we neglect the Holy Spirit and forget our confirmation, we are missing out on the very reason for our redemption. God became man not merely to save us *from* something (our sins), but to save us *for* something (to live as children of God). To be saved means nothing less than to share God's nature.

And so we do because of the gift of the Holy Spirit. Jesus told his apostles that the Spirit would "take what is mine and declare it to you" (Jn 6:14). It is the Spirit, then, who gives us our life in the Blessed Trinity. For it is the Spirit who gives us the life of the Son.

To send the Spirit was Jesus' stated purpose. He told his apostles: "It is to your advantage that I go away; for if I do not go away, the Counselor will not come to you; but if I go, I will send him to you . . . When the Spirit of truth comes, he will guide you into all the truth" (Jn 16:7, 13).

True to his promise, Jesus appeared to his apostles and "breathed on them, and said to them, 'Receive the Holy Spirit' " (Jn 20:22). Then, at the first Christian Pentecost, came a universal outpouring of the Holy Spirit upon the Church (Acts 2). This event had been foreshadowed in many Old Testament prophecies about the age of the Messiah (Is 44:3, 59:21; Ez 11:19, 36:25ff–27; Jl 2:28). Surely the greatness of the gift exceeded all expectation.

It was the gift not of something, but of Someone. It was the gift of the Holy Spirit.

It's clear from the Acts of the Apostles that Pentecost was an event intended for the entire Church, not just an elite, and not just for a day. It would be extended through time—institutionalized—by the sacraments. The gift of the Spirit came with baptism but was somehow completed by another rite. "Now when the apostles at Jerusalem heard that Samaria had received the word of God, they sent to them Peter and John, who came down and prayed for them that they might receive the Holy Spirit; for it had not yet fallen on any of them, but they had only been baptized in the name of the Lord Jesus. Then they laid their hands on them and they received the Holy Spirit" (Acts 8:14–17).

Tradition describes confirmation as the "seal" of the Holy Spirit. In the ancient world, to bear someone's seal, or wear it, was to be identified with that person, to be known as that person's child or servant. Confirmation marks us as God's own children. It confers a certain maturity upon us and empowers us to witness to the faith, defend the faith, and live responsibly within the Church. All these deeds are graces from God, and they do not depend upon our individual strengths or skills. The age at which a person is confirmed can vary widely from place to place. Some eastern churches confirm infants immediately after baptism, emphasizing the divine gratuity of the gift. Some western dioceses delay the sacrament until high-school matriculation or graduation, emphasizing that it is a sign of maturity, of coming into one's own in the Church. The Church teaches that confirmation, no matter when we receive it, "completes" our baptism.

We may wish to have received it at one age or another—earlier for the sake of the grace, or later for the sake of our understanding—but there's really no point to that. What we need to do is recognize that confirmation is a once-for-a-lifetime gift, and we can still call upon its grace every day of our lives. We have received all we need to reach spiritual maturity.

We receive what Christian tradition calls the "gifts of the Holy Spirit": wisdom, understanding, knowledge, counsel, piety, fortitude, and fear of the Lord. We also receive the fruits of the Holy Spirit, among them, for example: charity, joy, peace, patience, kindness, goodness, generosity, gentleness, faithfulness, modesty, self-control, and chastity.

When we see divisions in the Church—dissent, a lack of clarity, seemingly willful ignorance—then we see a need for the Holy Spirit. Rather than curse the darkness, we should invoke the third person.

We should examine ourselves on our devotion to the Holy Spirit and our appreciation for the day we were confirmed. Do we pray to the Holy Spirit as we pray to the Father and the Son? Do we pray to him personally? Because he is a person, not a force or an operation or an instrument.

If we are confirmed, then the Holy Spirit dwells within us. We are his temples (I Cor 6:19). We don't have to go far to get to know him.

Christ came to earth in order to give us the Spirit. He ascended to the Father so that the Spirit could descend on the Church. In these divine actions, salvation history manifested the divine processions. The Father sending the Son in history is an image of the Father generating the Son in eternity. The descent of the Spirit upon the Church at Pentecost is an image of the Spirit's procession from the Father and the Son in eternity.

So we must strive not to neglect or undervalue the Spirit's life in the Trinity, or our life in the Spirit. The Spirit's essential work is to reproduce Christ's life, suffering, death, and resurrection in each and all of us. If we neglect the Spirit, then we are neglecting Christ, too.

Ponder in Your Heart

Now that you have been "baptized into Christ" and have "put on Christ," you have become conformed to the Son of God (Gal 3:27; Rom 8:29). For God "destined us to be his sons" (Eph I:5) . . . Hence, since you "share in Christ" (Heb 3:14), it is right to call you Christs or anointed ones . . . You have become anointed ones by receiving the sign of the Holy Spirit. Since you are images of Christ, all the rites carried out over you have a symbolic meaning.

Christ bathed in the River Jordan, and having invested the waters with the divine presence of his body, he emerged from them, and the Holy Spirit visited him in substantial form, like coming to rest on like. In the same way, when you emerged from the pool of sacred waters you were anointed in a manner corresponding with Christ's anointing. That anointing is the Holy Spirit, of whom the blessed Isaiah spoke when he prophesied in the person of the Lord: "The Spirit of the Lord is upon me because he has anointed me" (Is 61:1) . . .

But be sure not to regard the [chrism] merely as ointment. Just as the bread of the Eucharist after the invocation of the Holy Spirit is no longer just bread, but the body of Christ, so the holy [chrism] after the invocation is no longer ordinary ointment but Christ's grace, which through the presence of the Holy Spirit instills his divinity into us.

—St. Cyril of Jerusalem, fourth century

20.

Marriage

I am not the first reader to note that the Bible is a book that tells a love story—the story of God's love for humankind. As if to emphasize the point, the Church arranged the Scriptures so that the biblical canon begins and ends with a wedding. In Genesis, the high point of the creation narrative is God's fashioning of man and woman, Adam and Eve, the primal two who become one flesh (Gen 2:23–24). In John's apocalypse, Revelation, the culmination is at the very end, in the seer's vision of heaven, which his angel guide describes as "the marriage supper of the Lamb" (Rev 19:9)—the celebration of the communion of Christ and his Church.

In between those two events, a love story unfolds. When God spoke through the prophets, he portrayed his covenant with Israel as a marriage. He spoke of himself, or his Messiah, coming as a bridegroom to take his people as his bride (see Hos 2:16–24; Jer 2:2; Is 54:4–8). Human marriage, then, was for Israel an earthly image of God's eternal love.

Some people wrongly caricature Israelite religion as "legalistic," simply because of its emphasis on the Law. But as Jon Levenson, a contemporary Jewish scholar, makes clear, "It is not a question of law *or* love, but law conceived in love, love expressed in law. The two are a unity." He goes on to explain that the Hebrew Scriptures are incomprehensible apart from this nuptial key: "What happened on the mountain in the ancient days was the consummation of a romance, a marriage in which YHWH was the groom and Israel . . . was the bride." Marriage got to the very meaning of the bond between God and his chosen people. It was a *covenant*—in Hebrew, *b'rith*—a family bond.

The joy, however, was not only for Israel. For all creation is caught up in the celebration of this "wedding" of heaven and earth. Through the prophet Hosea, God promises: "I will make for you a covenant on that day with the beasts of the field, the birds of the air, and the creeping things of the ground; and I will abolish the bow, the sword, and war from the land; and I will make you lie down in safety. And I will betroth you to me for ever; I will betroth you to me in righteousness and in justice, in steadfast love, and in mercy. I will betroth you to me in faithfulness; and you shall know the Lord" (2:18–20). Levenson concludes: "In the last stanza of Hosea's prophecy (vv. 23–25), all creation joins in the wedding ceremony. Sky responds to earth, and earth responds by bringing forth her bounty . . . The entire universe takes part in the sacred remarriage of YHWH and Israel."

Rabbi Michael Fishbane traces the influence of marital imagery from Hosea to Jeremiah (see Jer 2:2, 3:1). But, above all, he writes: "The topic of covenantal love between God and Israel came to celebrated expression in the classical rabbinic interpretations of the Song of Songs." Which tradition, a Christian might add, is found in the continuation of the Church's saints and scholars, from St.

Hippolytus and St. Gregory of Nyssa through St. Bernard of Clairvaux and St. Thomas Aquinas to Pope John Paul II.

The prophets foretold a new and everlasting covenant, which would be a renewal of the original covenant between God and Adam, God and humankind, God and all creation. It would, in fact, be so all encompassing as to be a "new creation." The imagery of the prophets, which was employed in turn by Jesus Christ, was the imagery of betrothal and marriage. Thus, when Jesus came, he called himself the "bridegroom" and those who were united to him in baptism were called "espoused" (see Jn 3:29; Mk 2:19; Mt 22:1–14, 25:1–13; 1 Cor 6:15–17; 2 Cor 11:2).

It is Jesus who gave us the first explicitly marital interpretation of Genesis. The word "marriage," after all, does not appear in the story of Adam and Eve. Yet, we know the story is about marriage because Jesus said it was (see Mk 10:2–16). Jesus said that the Genesis story reflects God's will "from the beginning of creation" and that "what God has joined together, no human being must separate."

Further along in the New Testament, St. Paul provided a profound mystical commentary. In his Letter to the Ephesians, he quoted the Genesis text and explained that this marriage covenant in the Garden is a reference to the covenant between "Christ and the Church" (see Eph 5:21–33). In using this unquestionable allusion to Adam and Eve becoming one flesh, Paul seems also to be shedding light on Adam's task and failure. He helps us see that Adam did *not* "give himself up" for his bride as he should have; instead, he allowed himself to be intimidated by the serpent. St. Paul helps us to see that Christ, on the other hand, does indeed "give himself up" for his bride, the Church. Where the first Adam had failed, with dire consequences, the new Adam succeeded, with saving power.

Note that Paul does not cancel out the literal meaning of the Genesis text, nor does he say it is not *truly* about real-world husbands and wives. In fact, he gives a beautiful teaching on the love that husbands and wives share. He is telling us, however, that marriage is also a symbol of a far greater mystery—the love that Christ has for his bride, the Church, the love that God has for his people.

This mystery receives its most powerful expression in the last book of the Bible, the Revelation of St. John, otherwise known as the Apocalypse—from the Greek word *apokalypsis,* which literally means "unveiling." Like the story of Adam and Eve, the Apocalypse evokes images that are both nuptial and priestly. Veils were then, as now, a standard part of a bride's wardrobe. The bride's "unveiling" was the culmination of the Jews' traditional weeklong wedding feast. Indeed, *apokalypsis* became associated with the first moment of marital intimacy and bodily communion, the physical consummation of the nuptial covenant.

Like a bride, God's sanctuary was veiled, to be unveiled only with the consummation of the New Covenant (see Mk 15:38). The holy of holies in Jerusalem's Temple was a four-square room, overlaid with gold (1 Kgs 6:19–20). It was shielded from sight by a floor-to-ceiling veil, a curtain embroidered with animal and floral decorations. (Thus, nature itself appeared as the symbolic "veil" of an even greater reality.) Yet the veil was torn, literally and symbolically, when Christ's body was torn in his act of self-giving love on the cross. Because of his self-offering, "we have confidence to enter the sanctuary by the blood of Jesus, by the new and living way which he opened for us through the veil, that is, through his flesh" (Heb 10:19–20).

That which is veiled is holy, to be unveiled only in covenant love. What the Apocalypse "unveils" is history's final consummation, the marriage of Christ to his bride, the Church (see Rev 19:9,

21:9, 22:17). She is "the holy city, New Jerusalem, coming down out of heaven from God, prepared as a bride adorned for her husband" (Rev 21:2). Like the holy of holies, Christ's bride is four-square and resplendent with pure gold (Rev 21:16–18).

By "unveiling" the Church, our priestly Bridegroom reveals the gift of his love to his bride—the New Jerusalem—in the "glory and beauty" of the Spirit (see Ex 28:2). The marriage inaugurates a new creation—"a new heaven and a new earth" (Rev 21:1).

It is a reprise of the opening chapters of Genesis. The third-century scholar Origen held that John's Apocalypse was the interpretive key to John's Gospel. Indeed, many puzzling aspects of the wedding feast at Cana seem to clear up when we understand that John is describing a new Genesis, a new creation, an eschatological "wedding feast" of the Lamb of God.

In the first covenant, we saw the marriage union of a man and a woman, Adam and Eve (see Gen 2:23–24). In the New Covenant, we see a new man and a new woman present at a wedding feast. True, Mary is Jesus' mother, not his bride. But in order to understand the supernatural depths of biblical symbolism that John intends here, we need to set aside our "natural" ways of reading. As the "woman," Mary becomes the locus of a host of biblical symbols and expectations. She is simultaneously a daughter of Israel, the mother of the new people of God, and the bride of God.

At Cana, Jesus appears as a New Adam, the firstborn of a new creation. What John implies is made clear elsewhere in the New Testament. Paul calls Jesus a "type" of Adam (see Rom 5:14) and the new or last Adam (see 1 Cor 15:21–22, 45–49). At Cana, Mary is the New Eve, the bride of the New Adam, the mother of the new creation.

At Cana comes the changing of water into wine—a transubstantiation that foreshadows Jesus' New Covenant meal: the Eucharist, the bodily consummation of the covenant between God and his Church. It is in the Eucharist that Jesus gives us his Body as food (Jn 6:26–58), and we, God's children, "share in flesh and blood" (Heb 2:14). It is in the Eucharist that Jesus draws all humanity to the marriage supper of the Lamb. It is in the Eucharist that Christ can look upon the Church as Adam looked upon Eve and say, "This at last is bone of my bones and flesh of my flesh" (Gen 2:23).

In the Eucharist we are made members of the wedding, each of us seated at the head table of the "marriage feast" that Jesus called "my banquet" in his parables. In the Eucharist, we enter into the depths of the communion of love that God intends for each person. In baptism, each of us is "betrothed to Christ" (2 Cor 11:2). Every Eucharist is our nuptial feast. "Every celebration," Augustine said, "is a celebration of marriage—the Church's nuptials are celebrated. The King's Son is about to marry a wife and . . . the guests frequenting the marriage are themselves the Bride . . . For all the Church is Christ's bride."

It is true of the Temple, and it is true of the bride. The connection is eminently clear in Jesus' mother tongue. The Hebrew word for holiness is *kiddushin,* which is also the word used for the Jewish wedding ceremony and for the state of matrimony.

When I first saw my beloved Kimberly on our wedding day, her beauty, even veiled, nearly knocked me off my feet. It was something mysterious, so much more than I could have expected. That wedding was a revelation to me. Little did I know that it was only a beginning, a genesis, a new creation, a new covenant.

Ponder in Your Heart

Marriage has God for its Author, and was from the very beginning a kind of foreshadowing of the incarnation of his Son; and therefore there abides in it something holy and religious; not extraneous, but innate; not derived from men, but implanted by nature.

—Pope Leo XIII, nineteenth century

21.

Priesthood

Before I was Catholic, I was anti-Catholic. As a high-school student I was active in para-church organizations that trained members to point out biblical "objections" to the Catholic faith. I often confronted Catholics with the words of Jesus: "call no man your father on earth" (Mt 23:9). Why then, I would ask, do Catholics address their priests as "Father"? I cringe now, not so much at my misunderstanding of Catholicism as my misunderstanding of the Bible.

After years of researching and praying, it became clear to me that the Scriptures indeed present God's priests as fathers. In biblical religion, a priest *is* a father—and even more a father than the man you or I might already call by that name "on earth," our natural or adoptive dads.

Let's begin at the beginning. In studying the Old Testament, we can divide the history of the priesthood into two periods: the patriarchal and the Levitical. The patriarchal period corresponds to the book of Genesis, while the Levitical period begins in Exodus and lasts until the coming of Jesus.

The religion of the patriarchal period was significantly different from the religion practiced by Israel after Moses received the Law on Mount Sinai. Patriarchal religion was firmly based on the natural family order, most especially the authority handed down from father to son—ideally the firstborn—often in the form of the "blessing" (see Gen 27).

In the book of Genesis, we find no separate priestly institution or caste. There is no temple set aside as the exclusive site of sacrifice. The patriarchs themselves build altars and present offerings at places and times of their own choosing (see Gen 4:3–4, 8:20–21, and 12:7–8). Fathers are empowered as priests by nature.

There are vestments associated with the office. When Rebekah took the garments of Esau, her firstborn, and gave them to Jacob (Gen 27:15), she was symbolically transferring the priestly office. We see the same priestly significance, a generation later, in the "long robe" that Jacob gave to his son Joseph (see Gen 37:3–4), and we understand why Joseph's half brothers were filled with envy.

Fatherhood is the original basis of priesthood. The very meaning of priesthood goes back to the father in the family—his representative role, spiritual authority, and religious service. The firstborn is the father's heir apparent, the one groomed to succeed one day to paternal authority and priesthood within the family. From the beginning, priesthood belonged to fathers and their "blessed" sons.

The pattern continued into the book of Exodus. There God declared to Moses, "Israel is my firstborn son" (Ex 4:22)—that is, among the many peoples of the earth, Israel was God's heir and his priest. At the Passover, the nation's firstborn sons were redeemed by the blood of the Paschal Lamb, and so they were consecrated to serve as priests within each of the twelve tribes and families of Israel (Ex 19:22–24). God gave Israel a unique vocation to be a "holy nation and a royal priesthood"—an "elder brother" in the family of nations. As the firstborn sons were to be priests in the family, so Israel was to act as God's firstborn son among the nations.

Still, there was a catch. Israel's status depended upon the biggest "if" in history: "if you obey my voice and keep my covenant" (Ex 19:5–6). In this, Israel failed. When the people worshipped the golden calf, the tribes of Israel forfeited the blessing of priesthood to one tribe, the Levites (Ex 32:25–29). For only the Levites resisted the temptation to idolatry.

Israel's priesthood thus became a hereditary office reserved to a cultural elite, and the home was no longer the primary place of priesthood and sacrifice. God had essentially "defrocked" the other tribes because of their infidelity. The Levites alone retained exclusive hold on Israel's priesthood through all the succeeding centuries, until the time of Jesus.

Even so, we can see in the book of Judges that Israel still identified priesthood with fatherhood. In the seventeenth chapter, we learn of a man named Micah, who consecrates his son a priest for the purpose of worship in the family's domestic shrine.

Yet, when a Levite appears at Micah's door, Micah pleads, "Stay with me, and be to me a father and a priest" (Jgs 17:10). A chapter later, Micah's plea is echoed, almost verbatim, by the Danites as they invite the Levite to be priest for their entire tribe: "Come with us, and be to us a father and a priest" (Jgs 18:19).

What's most remarkable about those requests is not what they assert, but what they assume. In just a few words, Micah provides us a rare glimpse of a transitional period for the people of Israel. Fathers were still installing their sons as priests in the domestic sanctuary—a custom left over from an earlier age. Yet the Levite's priesthood was already preferred to that of Micah's son—a hint of the newly emerging sacred order.

In the statement of Micah, and its repetition by the Danites, we also see that fatherhood was still considered an essential attribute of priestly ministry—even after priesthood had passed out of the family structure.

Those snippets from Judges are revealing. How embedded in the history of our religion—going back to its Israelite roots!—is this overarching reality of the spiritual paternity of the priest.

In the fullness of time, God the Father sent Jesus as a faithful firstborn son (Heb 1:6) and a priest (Heb 10:21)—not only to restore the natural priesthood, but also to establish a supernatural priesthood within the divine family, the Church.

Thus, with Jesus came a restoration of the natural priesthood of fathers and the establishment of a fatherly order of New Covenant priests. According to the Epistle to the Hebrews, Jesus' role and identity as the faithful firstborn Son of God (see Heb 1:6) qualify him as the perfect mediator between God, his Father, and us, his brothers and sisters. To Christ, we are "the children God has given me" (Heb 2:13), the "many sons" (Heb 2:10), "his brethren" (Heb 2:12), the new "seed of Abraham" (Heb 2:16), who together form God's "family/household," which Jesus builds and rules (Heb 3:3) as a son (Heb 3:6). As all Christians are identified with Christ, the Church becomes the "assembly of the firstborn" (Heb 12:23).

St. Peter, speaking to the Church, takes up the standard that Israel had lost in the desert: "You are a chosen race, a royal priesthood, a holy nation, God's own people" (1 Pet 2:9).

Now, once again, priests are fathers in the Church, which has now become "the universal family of God" (see CCC, nn. 1 and 1655). The apostles, who were Christ's first priests, clearly saw their own role as paternal. St. Paul asserts his spiritual fatherhood: "For though you have countless guides in Christ, you do not have many fathers. For I became your father in Christ Jesus through the gospel" (1 Cor 4:15; see also Phil 2:22; 1 Tim 1:2, 1:18; 2 Tim 1:2; Tit 1:4; Phlm 10). Paul was a father not because he was married and reared a family; he did not. He was a father because he was a priest: "a minister . . . in the priestly service of the gospel" (Rom 15:16).

St. Augustine looked the same way upon the episcopal office he had inherited from the apostles: "The apostles were sent as fathers; to replace those apostles, sons were born to you who were constituted bishops . . . The Church calls them fathers, she who gave birth to them, who placed them in the sees of their fathers . . . Such is the Catholic Church. She has given birth to sons who, through all the earth, continue the work of her first Fathers."

That is the true biblical teaching. Our priests are so much more than managers or functionaries. They are fathers. The sacramental priesthood is not so much a ceremonial function as it is a family relation.

Thus, my pastor is father to a large family. Before God, he must take responsibility for thousands of people. His fatherhood is not merely metaphorical. True fatherhood involves the communication of life. As a natural father, I have communicated biological human life—but, in the sacraments of baptism and Eucharist, a priest communicates *divine life* and the *divine humanity* of Jesus Christ.

Because of his spiritual fatherhood, an ordained priest requires our respect—*every* priest, in spite of his weaknesses or sins. When God said, "Honor your father and your mother," he didn't qualify the commandment. He gave no exceptions. When a man fails in priesthood, we should pray for him, confront him privately with our concerns, confront him with other witnesses; and, if all other attempts fail, we should take our case to the bishop, all the while honoring the man, his priesthood, and his fatherhood. This is what children do for their fathers (see Gen 9:22–27).

Ponder in Your Heart

The reason that God—loving men of old—had for begetting children is no longer cited because the begetting of children no longer has this meaning for us, since we can observe with our own eyes how, by the help of God, thousands of nations and peoples from cities, lands, and fields come and gather through the evangelical teaching of our Redeemer, to attend together the divine instruction through the evangelical teaching. It is appropriate for the teachers and heralds of the true worship of God that they are now free of all the chains of earning a living and daily cares. Indeed, for these men it is now commanded to distance themselves resolutely from marriage so as to devote themselves to a more important matter. Now they are concerned with a holy and not a carnal begetting of descendants. And they have taken upon themselves the begetting, the God-pleasing education, and the daily care, not only of one or two children, but of an indeterminable number all at once.

—Eusebius of Caesarea, fourth century

22.

Anointing of the Sick

When Jesus commissioned the Twelve, they went out into the world and saw immediate results. In St. Mark's Gospel we learn that they "anointed with oil many that were sick and healed them" (Mk 6:13). They must have been astonished at the power flowing through them. Yet it was a mere shadow of the task that still lay ahead for them. For, as Jesus made clear elsewhere in St. Mark's Gospel, it is a greater work to forgive sins than to heal even the gravely ill (Mk 2:9).

Jesus healed people with dire illnesses and disabilities as a sign of spiritual healing: "that you may know that the Son of man has authority on earth to forgive sin" (Mk 2:10). The physical signs were there for the sake of a spiritual reality. They were a concession to human weakness.

In fact, after the apostles had witnessed many such marvels, Jesus assured them that they would accomplish "greater works than these" (Jn 14:12).

In the beginning of their ministry, the apostles, like Jesus, restored bodily health. But it was a sign of the deeper healing they would accomplish, through the Church, after Pentecost.

We catch a glimpse of the Church's ministry of spiritual healing in the Letter of St. James: "Is any among you sick? Let him call for the elders [presbyters, or priests] of the Church, and let them pray over him, anointing him with oil in the name of the Lord; and the prayer of faith will save the sick man, and the Lord will raise him up; and if he has committed sins, he will be forgiven" (Jas 5:14–15).

This is the sacrament we know today as the anointing of the sick.

But it's fair for us to ask why *physical* illness should be an occasion for a *spiritual* healing. There are many good reasons, not least that grave physical suffering is often accompanied by difficult spiritual trial. When we are in extremis, we are far more likely to be tempted to doubt God's goodness and power—or even his existence. Job's wife sincerely expected her husband to give in to despair and "curse God" (Jb 2:9).

Sacramental anointing gives us the grace we need to face such trials. Consider what the symbol of oil suggested to the early Christians. Oil healed, and oil strengthened. It was a base for many medicines. It was also a liniment used by athletes in the arena. Olive oil was the rubdown that strengthened wrestlers for a contest and enabled them to slip away from the grip of their enemies.

All of these worldly values are symbolic of the anointing's spiritual value for Christians. It heals us spiritually, and it strengthens us spiritually, to slip away from the devil's grasp and endure our contest with him—and, more than endure, to prevail, to be "more than conquerors through him who loved us" (Rom 8:37). The anointing even brings about that great marvel that Jesus alluded to in St. Mark's Gospel: the forgiveness of sins. Thus we can face even certain death with a serene mind and peaceful conscience, in the reasonable hope that death will be our gateway to eternal life.

Sometimes, the sacramental anointing will bring about a physical healing as well, if healing will be conducive to the salvation of the soul. That's wonderful, but unusual; and actually, it's far less a marvel than the sacrament's ordinary effects. Anointing is far more likely to give us what we really need: humble acceptance of our suffering, in union with the suffering of Christ and in atonement for sins, especially our own. Anointing helps us transform physical suffering into something more deeply remedial, something truly redemptive.

This was Christ's great gift to his suffering people: a more perfect share in his life. The early Church recognized the gift and showed tremendous gratitude. We find the sacrament extolled among the Syriac-speaking Christians by their great pioneer, St. Aphrahat. We find it praised in Egypt by St. Serapion, the companion of St. Athanasius. We find Pope Innocent I giving the Roman clergy detailed instructions for administering the sacrament.

Jesus came to bring *salvation,* a word that, in the ancient languages, is synonymous with "health." His physical cures were outward signs of a deeper and more lasting spiritual healing. Presumably, all the people he cured during his ministry died of normal causes. Presumably, then, their physical cure was of secondary importance, subordinate to an enduring healing, a spiritual healing, that would survive even the death of the body.

Though his healings were primarily spiritual, Jesus still worked them by physical means—for example, by smearing a man with mud and spittle (Jn 9:6–7). Why would God manifest his power by such humble, earthy means? He made us, and so he knows that we human beings learn through sensible signs and sacraments.

Moreover, he intended his work not just for his small number of contacts in an obscure land, in the brief time of his ministry. He established the Church on earth so that he could extend his incarnation—his healing, his salvation—through time and space.

Ponder in Your Heart

The Old and the New Testament give an important place to sickness and its healing, teaching us to see the relationship of both to the economy of salvation. Sickness is connected with sin and the devil; when God heals bodies, it is to care for souls as well; healing the sick, together with freeing those possessed by demons, is one of the signs of the reign of the Messiah.

It is by sin that sickness came into the world, with the pain of drudgery, the sufferings of childbirth, and death (Gen 3:15–19). Although sickness is not expressly mentioned in the curse of Adam and Eve, theological tradition has always rightly seen it as included . . .

Though Christ healed the sick and gave his Church power over disease, he did not abolish sickness. Neither has he abolished death, pain, or drudgery. However, like death, sickness has been conquered; the messianic era has been established once and for all. In the heavenly Jerusalem these ills will have no place; here below they still exist. But Christ has overcome sin and Satan, the cause of sin. Sickness has therefore lost its quality of being a curse. It can become redemptive, enabling the Christian to become like Christ in his passion and at the same time to witness to the power of the risen Christ in him. When Paul begged to be delivered from the sting that attacked his body, the Lord answered:

"My strength will find scope in your weakness" (2 Cor 12:9). In his own flesh Paul is to accomplish for the Church "what is lacking to the sufferings of Christ" (Col 1:24). "We bear at all times in our body the sufferings of the death of Jesus, that the life of Jesus also may be manifested in our body" (2 Cor 4:10).

—Aimé Georges Martimort, twentieth century

VI

Spice of Life

23.

INCENSE

Catholicism is sometimes called the religion of "bells and smells." Our tradition engages the whole person. God created us as a unity of body and soul, and we return ourselves entirely to him in worship. We worship him in spirit and truth (Jn 4:24); and in our "spiritual worship" we "present our bodies" too "as a living sacrifice" (Rom 12:1). Thus, the Church's worship engages all that we are, including our bodily and spiritual senses. In the liturgy, we contemplate the Gospel, but that's not all. We hear it, see it, feel it, taste it, and smell it as well. We ring bells to herald the Lord's appearance. We burn fragrant incense before his altar.

I remember the first time I attended a Catholic liturgical event, a vespers service at a Byzantine seminary. My Calvinist background had not prepared me for the experience—the incense and icons, the prostrations and bows, the chant and the bells. All my senses were engaged. Afterward a seminarian asked me, "What do you think?" All I could say was "Now I know why God gave me a body: to worship the Lord with his people in liturgy."

Our worship is not merely good and true. It is beautiful. We make it beautiful because it is for God. A generation or two ago, incense was used much more commonly in the Mass. I am not the first convert to confess that he was enchanted by his initial experience of incense. It was a pleasant experience, an aesthetic experience. There is good reason why non-Catholics came to associate us with bells and smells. They make a powerful impression.

So powerful, in fact, that some people worried whether incense was a distraction from true worship. They worried that it might reduce liturgy to a merely aesthetic experience, a religion of externals rather than true interior life. God had warned the Israelites against such pomp; and, through the prophet Isaiah, he even went so far as to tell them: "Bring no more vain offerings; incense is an abomination to me" (Is 13:1).

Yet God was not abolishing external forms of worship. He wanted his people to cease neglecting their interior dispositions. In fact, through the prophet Malachi, he foretold a day when "from the rising of the sun to its setting . . . in every place incense is offered to my name, and a pure offering" (Mal 1:11).

Indeed, incense was an important part of biblical religion—and it remains so—because God himself took care to make it so. The offering of incense was an essential duty of the priests of the Old Covenant, and the ancient law took special care to prescribe its fragrances, vessels, and rites (see, for example, Exodus, chapter 30). Of the high priest Aaron, God said: "I chose him out of all the tribes of Israel to be my priest, to go up to my altar, to burn incense" (1 Sam 2:28).

And so the priests did, from the time of Moses to the time of Jesus, and beyond. Jesus' kinsman Zechariah was performing his priestly duty, burning incense in the Temple, when the angel

Gabriel appeared to him. It was apparently customary for a "whole multitude of the people" to pray nearby "at the hour of incense" every day (see Lk 1:9–11).

Incense became the most emblematic form of worship. Grains of incense, once dropped into a thurible with hot coals, rise heavenward as fragrant smoke. It's meant to be an outward sign of the inner mystery that is true prayer. "Let my prayer be counted as incense before you," said the Psalmist (Ps 141:2). The metaphor still worked for St. Paul (see Phil 4:18). A Jewish theologian of the first century, Philo of Alexandria, saw the freedom of the censer's smoke rising heavenward as a symbol of mankind's spiritual and rational qualities, fashioned after the divine image. When incense was offered with animal sacrifice, he said, it symbolized the entirety of human nature, body and soul, given to God.

So closely was incense associated with worship that, for the prophets, the very image of infidelity was to burn incense to idols. "I will utter my judgments against them, for all their wickedness in forsaking me; they have burned incense to other gods, and worshipped the works of their own hands" (Jer 1:16).

That image, too, worked just as well in the early centuries of Christianity, when Roman law required all citizens to burn incense before the emperor's protector deity. In offering the pinch of incense, some Christians saved their lives (temporarily), but committed the mortal sin of apostasy. They abandoned true worship for false; and, in doing so, they excommunicated themselves from the Church. The Christian who remained true referred to the traitors as "thurifers"—incense burners.

Thus, for all the ancients, to burn incense was to offer a richly symbolic act of worship. When St. John the Seer wanted words to depict the worship of the angels in heaven, he described it as attended by the rising smoke of much incense (see Rev 5:8). The prayers of the saints on earth, he says, rise as incense to heaven (see Rev 8:3–4).

Incense belongs with worship. It is not necessary, but it is beautiful and expressive, and worthy of divine worship. God prescribed it in the Law, not for *his* sake, but for ours, so that we might see, through this sign, the beauty of worship.

In the time of Jesus, incense was burned not only in the Temple, but also in the "communion" meal, the *chaburah* we discussed in chapter 4. The rabbis debated, at great length, the proper use of incense in this ritual of hearth and home.

How much more should we take care to incorporate this aromatic sign in the Mass—the meal of our New Covenant fellowship.

The earliest Christian documents—the *Didache,* St. Justin, St. Irenaeus—applied the prophecy of Malachi 1:11 to the Eucharist. The Holy Mass, they said, was the pure offering, the always-and-everywhere offering of incense to the God of Israel. St. Paul said it well: "But thanks be to God, who in Christ always leads us in triumph, and through us spreads the fragrance of the knowledge of him everywhere. For we are the aroma of Christ to God among those who are being saved . . . a fragrance from life to life" (2 Cor 2:14–16).

Ponder in Your Heart

Sovereign Lord Jesus Christ, O Word of God, who freely offered yourself a blameless sacrifice upon the cross to God the Father, the coal of double nature, that touched the lips of the prophet with the tongs and took away his sins: touch also the hearts of us sinners, and purify us from every stain, and present us holy beside your holy altar, that we may offer you a sacrifice of praise. Accept from us, your unprofitable servants, this incense as a sweet-smelling fragrance, make fragrant the evil odor of our soul and body, and purify us with the sanctifying power of your all-holy Spirit . . .

Accept from the hands of us sinners this incense, as you accepted the offering of Abel, and Noah, and Aaron, and Samuel, and of all your saints, guarding us from everything evil, and preserving us for continually pleasing, worshipping, and glorifying you . . .

We render thanks to you, the Savior and God of all, for all the good things you have given us, and for the communion of your holy and pure mysteries. We offer you this incense, praying: Keep us under the shadow of your wings, and count us worthy till our last breath to partake of your holy rites for the sanctification of our souls and bodies, for the inheritance of the kingdom of heaven. For you, O God, are our sanctification, and we send up praise and thanksgiving to You, Father, Son, and Holy Spirit.

—Prayers of Incense, from the Divine Liturgy of St. James, fourth century or earlier

24.

Candles

When the people of Israel offered worship in the Old Testament, they did so amid the flicker of many lights. "So Solomon made . . . the lampstands of pure gold, five on the south side and five on the north, before the inner sanctuary" (I Kgs 7:48–49). So important were these candelabra that the main one, the Temple menorah, became the most recognizable symbol of Judaism. It appears on countless coins, amulets, and house lamps from antiquity. When the Roman emperor Titus wished to memorialize his conquest of Jerusalem, he did so with an image of his troops carrying away the menorah.

We have every indication that the apostles saw their Eucharist in continuity with the worship of the Temple. It presented itself, in fact, as the fulfillment of Temple worship. This is evident in the cultic language used by the Apostolic Fathers (e.g., *sacrifice, offering,* and *altar*); and it is recognized by Jewish as well as Christian biblical scholars. In his commentary on Leviticus, Baruch Levine wrote: "Christian worship in the form of the traditional mass affords the devout an experience of sacrifice, of communion, and proclaims that God is present. The Christian church, then, is a temple."

The generation of the apostles observed that continuity in many ways, employing in the liturgy many of the details formerly associated with Temple worship. This is evident in the New Testament treatment of lights and lamps.

In one of history's earliest descriptions of Christian liturgy, we find St. Paul preaching in a crowded room. St. Luke notes that "There were many lights in the upper chamber where we were gathered" (Acts 20:8). So many lights in such a small space would be tremendous overkill—unless they served ceremonial rather than utilitarian purposes.

When we arrive at the Apocalypse, at the close of the New Testament Scriptures, St. John shows us the worship of heaven in images that consistently reflect earthly worship. Everywhere there are lamp stands. The lights shine as a symbol of the life of the Church. If a Church is falling slack in its devotion, John warns that God could remove its lamp stand (see Rev 2:5). In a stunning liturgical image, Christ appears, vested as a priest, amid the light of many lamps (Rev 1:12–13). Surely, this was a familiar image—that of the Christian clergy who offered the liturgy "in the person of Christ" (*en prosopo Christou,* 2 Cor 2:10).

The lamp was itself a symbol of Jesus Christ, who consistently spoke of his Gospel and even of himself in terms of light. "I am the light of the world; he who follows me will not walk in darkness, but will have the light of life" (Jn 8:12). *Illumination* (sometimes rendered "enlightenment") was among the early Church's most common synonyms for baptism (see Heb 10:32). Still today, on the Church's great celebration of baptism, the Easter Vigil liturgy, the priest holds aloft the paschal candle and proclaims "Christ our light!" three times.

The lamp is a symbol of Christ, God's presence among us. Yet it is still more. Christ came not just to light our way, but to give us his light as our own. The God-man who revealed himself to be the light of the world also told his followers: "You are the light of the world" (Mt 5:14). So closely are Christians identified with Christ that we come, through illumination, to be lights ourselves. We are partakers of the divine light (2 Pt 1:4); by grace it becomes our nature, too! Thus we can truly sing: *This little light of mine, I'm gonna let it shine.*

The early Church Fathers attest to the abundant use of lights in Christian worship, far beyond mere functionality. The greatest Scripture scholar in the ancient world, St. Jerome, delighted in this custom of the Church: "whenever the Gospel is to be read the candles are lighted—although the dawn may be reddening the sky—*not of course to scatter the darkness, but by way of showing our joy.*"

Again, the candles represent the light of Christ, but it is a light he has shared with his chosen people, his saints. Jerome notes that Jesus described St. John the Baptist as "a burning and shining lamp" (Jn 5:35). Thus, Christians, even today, follow the example of Jesus as we light candles at the chapels of the saints. Jerome recalls the funeral of a holy woman, St. Paula, whose body was attended in procession by many bishops bearing lights. He also describes the numerous wicks that burned at the shrines of the martyrs. And still today, we burn candles at the shrines of the saints. We join our prayers with theirs.

St. Athanasius of Alexandria referred to the lighting of votive candles as an "offering" of the faithful. When many of them are alight—whether before an image of Jesus, or Mary, or the saints—it gives great glory to God, who has shared his glory with us. St. Paulinus of Nola described such a shrine in the late fourth century: "With crowded lamps are these bright altars crown'd, and waxen tapers shedding perfume round / from fragrant wicks, beam calm a scented ray / to gladden night, and joy e'en radiant day . . . countless lamps in never-ending blaze."

Said St. Jerome: "Under the figure of material light, that light is represented of which we read in the Psalter, 'Your word is a lamp unto my feet, O Lord, and a light unto my paths' (Ps 119:105)." That light is Christ. And by grace it is his saints, too. It's you, and it's me.

Let it shine, let it shine, let it shine!

Ponder in Your Heart

The lamps that you kindle are a sacrament of the illumination [of baptism] by means of which we shall meet the Bridegroom as shining and virgin souls, with the lamps of our faith shining, not sleeping through our carelessness, that we may not miss him that we look for if he come unexpectedly; nor yet unfed, and without oil, and destitute of good works, that we be not cast out of the bridal chamber [see Mt 25:1–13]. For I see how pitiable is such a case. He will come when the cry demands the meeting, and those who are prudent shall meet him, with their light shining and its food abundant.

—St. Gregory Nazianzen, fourth century

25.

Sacred Images

A colossal mosaic, *Christ in Majesty,* dominates the great upper church at the Basilica Shrine of the Immaculate Conception in Washington, D.C. It is a fierce portrayal of Jesus, his passion restrained only by the fixity of the Byzantine style.

It's an image that resonates with me on many levels. Through my earliest years as a Christian—through my teens, through college and through seminary preparation for Presbyterian ministry—my formation was overwhelmingly Calvinist, a Protestant tradition that emphasizes God's sovereignty and his judgment. "For the Lord is our judge, the Lord is our ruler, the Lord is our king," said the prophet Isaiah (Is 33:22). And that's how Jesus appears in the Basilica. The irony is that my Calvinist background prepared me to think of Christ that way, but not to *see* him that way—at least not in this life. The reformer John Calvin was a forceful opponent of devotional images, favoring bare church walls and even bare crosses. He held that images—even images of Christ—presented a temptation to idolatry, the worship of a temporal sign in place of the sovereign and transcendent Lord.

I am now more than two decades a Roman Catholic. Yet every time I kneel beneath that overpowering image I wonder whether it is my vestigial inner Calvinist that thrills at such an expression of God's sovereignty—thrilling, nevertheless, as only a Catholic can thrill before a sacred image.

Some years ago, an essayist nicknamed this icon "Scary Jesus." And it is a little scary. It certainly seems to violate the canons of the Christian greeting-card industry. Contemporary Christian images bid us imagine the Lord backing up the goalie in a junior-varsity soccer game, or hugging teens on prom night. In modern images, Jesus often looks like a nice guy Norman Rockwell somehow missed in all those *Saturday Evening Post* covers. "Scary Jesus" doesn't fit the profile.

Still, there is a more disquieting paradox at work in *Christ in Majesty*. The mosaic portrays Christ in judgment, as we might encounter him in the book of Revelation. Yet doesn't the same book portray Christ as a lamb, so gentle that he can pass for dead (Rev 5:6)? Didn't the Word become flesh as a man who blessed the meek and didn't fight back?

The icon forces us to confront a seeming contradiction in Christianity: our Lord is a just judge, a powerful vindicator, whose wrath is capable of consigning mortal sinners to hell; yet our Lord is merciful and as meek as a lowly barnyard animal in its infancy.

Some people have tried to reconcile these images by making them sequential. Jesus was soft and tender in his first coming, they say, but with the second coming the gloves will be off, and then it's no more Mr. Nice Guy. Well, this doesn't work for several reasons: first, because the Gospels show us that Jesus did indeed vent his wrath on wicked men during his earthly life; but also because the book of Revelation shows our Lord to be a lamb to the very end, at the consummation of all human history.

So which shall we worship? Which shall we contemplate? The Judge or the Lamb? Scary Jesus or Mr. Nice Guy? Which is the true Lord and Christ?

The dogmatic truth is that we need not choose. The mystery of the incarnation demands that we accept the perfect union of many seemingly incompatible things: the finite contains the infinite; the eternal enters time; the sacrificial lamb presides on the Day of Wrath.

This is not a subtlety reserved for theologians. Dockworkers and poultry keepers, washer women and seamstresses have known this since the birthday of the Church. Even Christians who couldn't read knew the truth of Christ because of sacred images like *Christ in Majesty.*

In the eighth century a movement arose in the eastern churches to do away with religious images. It was a movement of elites—intellectuals, theologians, and emperors. They thought that icons were an insult to God's glory and majesty, which cannot really be portrayed. The transcendent God should be worshipped only with the intellect, they said. They received an imperial license to destroy the icons in the churches; and for this they earned the name *iconoclasts,* image smashers.

The saints, however, opposed these elites, and the saints prevailed. These holy men and women called themselves *iconodules*—"those who honor icons." They argued that since God had condescended to take on flesh, the common people had the right to contemplate him enfleshed. The most eloquent of the iconodules, St. Theodore of Studion, wrote that Christ "does not abandon the exalted reality of his divinity, which is immaterial and cannot be circumscribed; and yet it is his glory to abase himself in such a noble manner down to our own level that now in his body he can be circumscribed. He has become matter, that is: flesh, he who sustains everything that exists; and he is not ashamed to have become what he has taken on, and to be called such."

What the face of the human Jesus revealed during his life on earth during the first century, sacred images reveal nowadays. Even when a picture portrays Christ as a ruler and judge, it portrays him as a human being and reminds us of his humility, his willingness to join in the human condition, with all its weaknesses. Throughout history, some people have been scandalized by God's assuming human flesh in Jesus—by his bleeding and dying. They wanted him safely back in his heaven as purely divine. But that cannot be, because, as John's Gospel reminds us, the Word was made flesh and dwelt among us—and he still has that flesh. He didn't shed it the way a snake sheds its skin when he died. He glorified that flesh and now offers it as love to the Father. What is scandalous about these images is simply the scandal of the incarnation, with all its paradoxes.

Ponder in Your Heart

Since some find fault with us for worshipping and honoring the image of our Savior and that of Our Lady, and those, too, of the rest of the saints and servants of Christ, let them remember that in the beginning God created man after his own image (Gen 1:26). On what grounds, then, do we show reverence to each other unless because we are made after God's image? For as

Basil, that much-versed expounder of divine things, says, the honor given to the image passes over to the prototype . . . Why was it that the Mosaic people honored the tabernacle (Ex 33:10) that bore an image and type of heavenly things, or rather of the whole creation? God indeed said to Moses, "See that you make them after the pattern for them, which is being shown you on the mountain" (Ex 25:40). The Cherubim, too, which overshadow the mercy seat, are they not the work of men's hands (Ex 25:18)? What, further, is the celebrated Temple at Jerusalem? Is it not handmade and fashioned by the skill of men (1 Kgs 8)? . . .

God in the depths of his pity became true man for our salvation . . . he lived upon the earth and dwelt among men (Bar 3:38), worked miracles, suffered, was crucified, rose again and was taken back to heaven. Since all these things actually took place and were seen by men, they were written for the remembrance and instruction of us who were not alive at that time, so that though we saw not, we may still, hearing and believing, obtain the blessing of the Lord. But not every one can read; nor does everyone have time for reading. So the Fathers gave their approval to depicting these events on images . . . in order that they should form a concise memorial of them. Often, doubtless, when we do not have the Lord's passion in mind and see the image of Christ's crucifixion, his saving passion is brought back to memory, and we fall down and worship not the material but that which is depicted—just as we do not worship the material from which the Gospels are made, nor the material of the cross, but that which these symbolize . . . It is just the same in the case of the mother of the Lord. For the honor we give her is referred to him who was made flesh from her . . . The honor rendered to the image passes over to the prototype.

—St. John of Damascus, eighth century

26.

Relics

So completely do the saints correspond to God's grace that—for a millennium and more after their bodies have lain lifeless—their very bones remain a channel of grace. Long before the coming of Christ, the prophet Ezekiel beheld a vision of a field of dry bones, and the Lord God said to the bones: "Behold, I will cause breath to enter you, and you shall live" (Ez 37:5). The Lord God breathed on the bones, and indeed they returned to life. Yet the breath of God accomplishes still more that that. It renders the bones of his chosen people not only *living*, but truly *life-giving.*

Consider another story from the age of the prophets. "And as a man was being buried, lo, a marauding band was seen and the man was cast into the grave of Elisha; and as soon as the man touched the bones of Elisha, he revived, and stood on his feet" (2 Kgs 13:21). By the mere touch of the prophet Elisha's lifeless bones, life returned to a dead man's body—so great is the grace of God as it works through the bodies of the saints. That principle was true in the Old Covenant as well as the New. The prophet Elisha understood it while he was still alive. Once, when he needed to cross a river, he simply struck the water with the garment of his master Elijah, and the waters parted before him (see 2 Kgs 2:14). By the time of Jesus, believers took the doctrine of relics for granted. In the Gospels we find a woman who "suffered from a hemorrhage for twelve years." Though she had given up on medical doctors, she knew she could trust in the touch of something that had touched the sacred. As Jesus passed by, she said to herself, "If I only touch his garment, I shall be made well" (Mt 9:20–21). And she was made well.

Before Jesus ascended to heaven, he breathed upon the Church (Jn 20:22) and imparted his life-giving Spirit. Thereby his healing ministry passed to the saints; and the New Testament shows them busy about it: "And more than ever believers were added to the Lord, multitudes both of men and women, so that they even carried out the sick into the streets, and laid them on beds and pallets, that as Peter came by at least his shadow might fall on some of them. The people also gathered from the towns around Jerusalem, bringing the sick and those afflicted with unclean spirits, and they were all healed" (Acts 5:14–16).

Decades passed, and still "God did extraordinary miracles by the hands of Paul, so that handkerchiefs or aprons were carried away from his body to the sick, and diseases left them and the evil spirits came out of them" (Acts 19:11–12).

All it took was the brush of an apostle's body, the touch of his hanky or apron—even just his shadow!

Is it any wonder that the early Christians continued to place great trust in the relics of the saints? Archaeologists have turned up ample evidence of this devotion, dating back to the deaths of

Saints Peter and Paul in Rome. The faithful took care to preserve their remains, and pilgrims streamed to the city to venerate them and touch them.

Nor did the Church reserve such veneration exclusively for the bones of the apostles. The early Christians built many churches over the graves of the martyrs. This was a decisive break with the traditions of the Romans and the Jews, who (like most ancient peoples) considered human corpses to be defiling and unclean—death-dealing rather than life-giving.

Yet Christians believed in the marvelous exchange: Christ became what we are so that we might become what he is. He came to divinize us, body and soul and flesh and bones and blood. So the bodies of the saints now convey his life to the world.

Christians celebrated that fact with great joy, great pomp, and great churches—St. Peter's Basilica, St. Paul's Outside the Walls: these are grand reliquary churches, built upon gravesites. The emperor Julian, who led the charge in the late fourth century to repaganize the Roman Empire, detested the Christians for their cult of relics: "you have filled the whole world with tombs and sepulchers," he said.

Inside the basilicas, the Church constructed its altars directly over the caskets of the apostles and martyrs. Over time, it became customary for all Catholic parishes to deposit small relics of the saints within a sealed cavity inside the church's altar. Thus, every Church on earth could follow, in a sensible way, after the spiritual worship St. John glimpsed in heaven: "When he opened the fifth seal, I saw under the altar the souls of those who had been slain for the word of God and for the witness they had borne" (Rev 6:9).

The Church's most precious relics, however, are those associated with Jesus' life and ministry, passion and death. Thus the whole of Christendom contributes for the care of the shrines in the Holy Land, where Jesus spent his earthly life. The Church of the Holy Sepulchre rises above Jesus' tomb, as the Church of the Nativity stands on the traditional site of his birth. Documents dating to the fourth century show the intensity of Christians' devotion to the wood of the true cross. In fact, sometimes people got carried away by their devotion. In ancient times, during Holy Week, the Bishop of Jerusalem would customarily call forth his congregation to kiss the relics of the true cross, and one year a man bit off a chunk before walking away!

So I'm emphatically *not* saying that the doctrine of relics was, always and everywhere, very clearly understood.

But as it was in the ancient Church, so it remains today: to venerate relics is something distinctly and characteristically Christian.

Ponder in Your Heart

[Addressed to a heretic, Vigilantius, who rejected the veneration of relics:]

Tell us more clearly—so that there may be no restraint on your blasphemy—what you mean by the phrase "a bit of powder wrapped up in a costly cloth in a tiny vessel."

It is nothing less than the relics of the martyrs that he is troubled to see covered with a costly veil, and not bound up with rags or hair-cloth, or thrown in the dump, so that Vigilantius alone in his drunken slumber may be worshipped.

Are we, therefore, guilty of sacrilege when we enter the basilicas of the apostles? Was the Emperor Constantius I guilty of sacrilege when he transferred the sacred relics of Andrew, Luke, and Timothy to Constantinople? In their presence the demons cry out (Acts 8:7, 5:16)—and the devils who dwell in Vigilantius confess that they feel the influence of the saints. And at the present day is the Emperor Arcadius guilty of sacrilege, who after so long a time has conveyed the bones of the blessed Samuel from Judea to Thrace? Are all the bishops to be considered not only sacrilegious, but silly into the bargain, because they carried that most worthless thing, dust and ashes, wrapped in silk in golden vessel? Are the people of all the churches fools, because they went to meet the sacred relics, and welcomed them with as much joy as if they beheld a living prophet in their midst, so that there was one great swarm of people from Palestine to Chalcedon with one voice re-echoing the praises of Christ? . . .

You show mistrust because you think only of the dead body, and therefore blaspheme. Read the Gospel: The God of Abraham, the God of Isaac, the God of Jacob: he is not the God of the dead, but of the living (Mt 22:32). If, then, they are alive, they are not, to use your expression, kept in honorable confinement.

—St. Jerome, fifth century

27.

Fasting and Mortification

You'll sometimes hear people say that fasting and bodily discipline are "outmoded" expressions of Catholic spirituality. But that's not true. As long as we follow Christ, we will have to deny our bodies the things they want. Jesus said: "If any man would come after me, let him deny himself and take up his cross and follow me" (Mt 16:24). St. Paul put it in stronger terms when he told the Colossians to "put to death therefore what is earthly in you" (Col 3:5).

All the things of the earth are good, because God has made them. Yet there's no doubt that our desire for many of them is out of whack. Given the opportunity, most of us will eat more than our bodies need, and that's not good for us. In fact, this may be worse for the soul than it is for the body. For we become attached to created things and to the pleasure they bring us. And in time, we prefer the pleasure to spiritual goods. We'd rather take a nap or watch a sitcom than pray the Rosary. We'd rather stay tuned to a talk radio host who amuses us, even though we know he tempts us to sin against charity when he belittles politicians. We eagerly take another beer, even though we know that our physician and our confessor are united in opposing this move.

St. Augustine said that sin begins as a turning away from God and a turning toward lesser goods. When we sin, we don't choose evil. We choose something less than God and his will.

Again, our bodies incline us this way. Ever since the sin of our first ancestors, our bodily appetites are disordered. So, as long as we have bodies, they will need to be disciplined. Our bodies want more than they need, so we must give them less than they want.

How do we do this? Our methods are not unlike the methods we use to obtain difficult earthly goals. If we want to get in shape, what do we do? We exercise. We diet. The harder we strive, the better the results. If we want to advance in our career, how do we go about it? We forgo pleasures and spend more time in concentrated work. Think of the slogans that drive us: "No pain, no gain." An accountant I know told me that the unofficial motto in his firm was: "Don't date—work late."

For earthly or heavenly goals, our bodies need discipline. Our bodies must be subject to our reason—or the order will be reversed: our reason will soon be subject to our bodies. The early Christians knew this, and they fasted frequently. St. Paul went even further: "I pommel my body and subdue it" (I Cor 9:27).

When we fast, we follow consistent biblical models. Moses and Elijah fasted before going into God's presence (Ex 34:28; I Kgs 19:8). Anna the prophetess fasted to prepare herself for the coming of the Messiah (Lk 2:37). Jesus fasted (Mt 4:2), even though he needed no purification. So he must have done this for the sake of our imitation. In fact, he assumed that we would follow his example. "When you fast," he said, "do not look gloomy like the hypocrites" (Mt 6:16). He did not say "*if* you fast," but "when."

The Church requires certain disciplines of us. We must fast for an hour before receiving Holy Communion. It's a small sacrifice, and it may even produce a "sacramental hunger" in us—not only a hunger for the sacrament, but a hunger that is itself a bodily sign of a spiritual reality: our desire for union with the Lord. Surely that's why the apostles fasted in preparation for the liturgy (see Acts 13:2–3).

We are required to make substantial fasts on two days every year, Ash Wednesday and Good Friday. On those days, we may take only one full meal, and that meal must not be greater than the other meals combined. On those two days, and on all the Fridays of Lent, we may not eat meat. (Actually, the Church suggests that we abstain from meat on all the Fridays of the year, or substitute some other sacrifice.)

Measured against the sacrifices we've made in other areas of life—school, work, parenting, even sports—these don't add up to much. But our faithfulness in these small renunciations should be an indicator of our constant fidelity to that daily self-denial that Jesus demands from us. We should make a habit of it, and give special preference to those sacrifices that make others happy: choosing the movie my spouse would rather see, or leaving the last portions of a snack for my children to enjoy.

By voluntary self-denial, we return to God what is his; and we demonstrate our preference for spiritual goods. In due course, we will lose the good things one by one. How much better for us if we give them up voluntarily, for love? If our self-denial is habitual, then perhaps we won't grow so bitter when age takes away our delights, as it certainly will, without asking our permission. The Catholic author Jorge Luis Borges wrote a story that symbolically depicted the limits of sensory pleasure. The narrator, an old man, dreams that our enjoyment of earthly pleasures is limited by a fated number: "You will use up the number that corresponds to ginger and you will go on living. You will use up the number that corresponds to the smoothness of crystal and you will go on living a few more days."

We will all face death someday. Some people face it with serenity and even joy, in expectation of fulfillment and gain. Others face it in misery because of their losses.

If all life is a preparation for the moment of death, Jesus' advice on daily self-denial indeed makes good sense. "So you have sorrow now, but I will see you again and your hearts will rejoice, and no one will take your joy from you" (Jn 16:22).

"When you fast," Jesus said, "do not look gloomy." And we who fast do have every reason to rejoice. When we live this way, we imitate Christ, who enjoyed perfect freedom because no one could take anything away from him. He had already voluntarily given up even himself (Jn 10:17).

Imitating him would be enough. But we do still more. We share his life and his divine work of redemption. We can apply the fruits of our self-denial to others, as an act of love. Like St. Paul, we can say: "Now I rejoice in my sufferings for your sake, and in my flesh I complete what is lacking in Christ's afflictions for the sake of his body, that is, the Church" (Col 1:24).

Ponder in Your Heart

Let us fall to fasting, to prayer, to almsgiving in time and give that unto God that may be taken from us. If the devil put in our mind the saving of our land and our goods, let us remember that we cannot save them long. If he fear us with exile and fleeing from our country, let us remember that we be born into the broad world, and not like a tree to stick in one place, and that whithersoever we go, God shall go with us.

—St. Thomas More, sixteenth century

VII

Abundant Life

28.

Confession

Confession is the way God's people have always gone about repenting, healing, and reconciling. Read the first pages of the Bible, and you'll find God asking Adam, "Where are you?" Later, God asks the murderer Cain, "Where is your brother?" The Almighty isn't looking for information. He already knows everything. He's looking for the one thing Adam or Cain should have given him, but didn't—and that's a full confession. He wanted it for their sake, so that they might live again in the truth. Unfortunately, it was not forthcoming.

Go through the rest of the Old Testament, however, and you'll find that God taught the people of Israel many ways to confess their sins and make amends—with sacrifices, sin offerings, and burnt offerings. It was hard work, expensive and bloody. A penitent had to buy his own animal, bring it to the altar, and slaughter it himself. But he could walk away with a certain peace of mind, having made his confession and completed the penance that God required.

The human need for confession didn't vanish with the coming of Jesus. But now it's fulfilled in a neater, easier, and more powerful way. Jesus responded to it perfectly, by establishing a ministry and a sacrament of penance in the Church.

There are many ways of looking at confession, and all of them are valid. You can look at it as a courtroom with a divine judge. You can look at it as an accounting of debts. I think it's most helpful to look at it as healing—as health care. Confession does for our souls what doctors, dieticians, physical therapists, and pharmacists do for our bodies.

Think about all we do to keep our bodies in working order. We go for regular checkups with a primary-care physician, a dentist, an eye doctor. And no one has to remind us to brush our teeth, take a shower, and pop the pills for whatever ails us. All this is good for us, and it's good for everyone around us, too. No one wants to work beside us if we decide to stop showering.

Well, if we spend so much effort on the care of our bodies, shouldn't we be spending more time on our souls? After all, our bodies will pass away soon enough, but our souls will live on forever.

What's more, our decisions about our spiritual health and hygiene will have a *tremendous* effect on the people around us. Nothing serves family life and workplace dynamics so well as a clean soul and the advice of a good confessor. On the other hand, nothing hurts our relationships and our mental health so much as the burden of sin and guilt. Confession is free health care, and free life insurance as well! Christ is the divine physician; and, unlike human physicians, he can guarantee us a cure every time. In fact, he can guarantee us immortality. Any doctor who could do all that would have long lines stretching from his office door. The thing that will make confession less intimidating is a stronger faith in Jesus Christ and what he can do for us.

When your body's hurting, you need to see a doctor. You might not *want* to see a doctor. You might not find doctor visits particularly pleasant. Maybe you even have a deep-seated fear of doctors' offices. But nothing else will do to set your broken limb, purge your body of a bug, or close up your bleeding wound. It won't help you to visit your accountant or your auto mechanic.

The New Testament rite differs from the Old because now God himself serves as high priest. The scribes and pharisees were right when they asked Jesus, "Who can forgive sins but God alone?" (Mk 2:7). What they would not believe was that Jesus is the Son of God. Only Jesus could say with authority: "My son, your sins are forgiven" (Mk 2:5).

Jesus had the authority to share that power with his chosen clergy, his apostles. And that's precisely what he did, on the day of his resurrection: "He breathed on them, and said to them, 'Receive the Holy Spirit. If you forgive the sins of any, they are forgiven; if you retain the sins of any, they are retained' " (Jn 20:22–23).

Jesus thus gave his apostles a power greater than that of Israel's priests. The rabbis referred to this ancient priestly power in terms of "binding and loosing," and Jesus used those very words to describe what he was giving to his disciples. For the rabbis, to bind or loose meant to judge someone to be in communion with the chosen people—or cut off from its life and worship.

In bringing this old office to its fulfillment, Jesus added a new dimension. No longer would the authorities pass a sentence that was merely earthly. Since the Church shared the power of God incarnate, her power would extend as far as the power of God. "Truly, I say to you, whatever you bind on earth shall be bound in heaven, and whatever you loose on earth shall be loosed in heaven" (Mt 18:18). The Church could forgive sins in God's name. The Church could lighten or waive the punishment that's due for sin.

All of that, however, presupposes a confession. Before the apostles could exercise their power over souls, they would need to hear sins confessed aloud. Otherwise, they could not know what to bind or loose.

The apostles exercised this authority and preached confession to the first Christians. "If we confess our sins, [God] is faithful and just," said St. John, "and will forgive our sins and cleanse us from all unrighteousness" (1 Jn 1:9). St. Paul makes the further clarification that "confession" is something you do "with your mouth," not just with your heart and mind (Rom 10:10). Paul considered his mission to be a "ministry of reconciliation" (2 Cor 5:18)—again, a role that had, in the Old Covenant, been carried out by the Jerusalem priests, who brought about the forgiveness of sins through the expiating sacrifices of the Temple.

St. James, for his part, took up the matter of confession at the end of his discussion of the sacramental duties of the clergy. The term he used for clergymen is the Greek *presbuterous,* which literally means "elders," but which is the root of the English word *priest.* Here's what James said: "Is any among you sick? Let him call for the elders of the Church, and let them pray over him, anointing him with oil in the name of the Lord; and the prayer of faith will save the sick man, and the Lord will raise him up; and if he has committed sins, he will be forgiven. Therefore confess your sins to one another, and pray for one another, that you may be healed" (Jas 5:14–16).

James is clearly setting the practice of confession in connection with the priest's healing ministry. Because priests are healers, we call upon them to anoint our bodies when we are physically ill; and, *therefore*, even more eagerly, we go to them for the healing sacrament of forgiveness when our souls are sick with sin.

Note that St. James does not exhort his congregation to confess their sins to Jesus alone; nor does he tell them to confess their sins silently, in their hearts. They may do all these things, and all to their credit, but they will not yet be faithful to the word of God preached by St. James—not until they confess their sins aloud to "another," and specifically to a *presbyter*, a priest.

All of this was clear to the earliest churches. It is the teaching we find in the *Didache*, the most ancient Christian document we possess apart from the Scriptures. There we read: "Thou shalt confess thy transgressions in the Church and shalt not come unto prayer with an evil conscience." A later chapter speaks of the importance of confession before receiving Communion: "On the Lord's Day gather together, break bread, and give thanks [in Greek, *eucharistesate*], first confessing your sins so that your sacrifice may be pure."

Confession should always be individual, auricular—that is, spoken—and specific. The Church approves communal penance services but clearly states that they should lead the individual believer to an individual confession. Even if you receive general absolution on the battlefield, you're supposed to get yourself to a priest as soon as you can when the bullets stop flying.

Not long ago, it was customary for devout Catholics to go to confession every week. The lines on Saturday were very long. The saints have recommended that we go at least once a month.

Why has the practice dwindled in recent years, with some parishes offering the sacrament "by appointment only"? Recent popes have attributed this decline to a loss of the sense of sin. I think that's true. Ours is a no-fault culture. We have no-fault auto coverage and no-fault divorce. We've convinced ourselves that "I'm okay, you're okay," no matter what choices we make in life.

Yet the fact is that we're not okay, because we all sin, and we all *suffer* from our own sins and the sins of others. Thus, we're out of sync with the God who made us and we're out of sync with the world he made for us. Yes, God loves us just the way we are, but he loves us too much to keep us that way. We need to experience his forgiveness so that we can heal, and grow, and then practice forgiveness ourselves.

We need to recover a healthy sense of sin, so that we can recover spiritual health.

Ponder in Your Heart

It is better to confess one's sins than to harden one's heart.

—Pope St. Clement I, first century

29.

Indulgences

Imagine that you loaned a thousand dollars to a friend, who then came back to you and said, "You'll never guess what happened. I was at the mall, and I lost all the money, and I can't repay you for at least six months." There would be tension, no doubt, and perhaps a strained relationship.

Now imagine that a good friend shows up and says to you: "I prayed for your debtor . . . so please release the debt." If a thousand dollars means as much to your budget as it means to mine, you might laugh out loud. The proposal would offend your sense of justice, and rightly so.

Some people try to portray indulgences that way—as the forgiveness of debt in the spiritual realm. But an indulgence is *not* the forgiveness of a debt. It's the *payment* of the debt. It's as if someone showed up and paid you the thousand dollars on behalf of your friend.

That's what Christ empowers Mary and the saints to do for us, and that's what Christ empowers us to do for others, even those who have died and are now in purgatory.

When we gain an indulgence, the Church draws from the treasury of merits of Christ and the saints—a treasury that is infinite—and applies those merits to us, assuming we are in the state of grace (we have not sinned grievously) and have fulfilled other conditions (confession, communion, and prayers for the pope). An indulgence may be plenary, remitting all the punishment due our sins, or partial.

It's an idea that is as old as biblical religion, and it has always been a part of biblical religion. The ancient rabbis bear witness to it, as do the Church Fathers. Let's consider it as we find it in the Old Testament.

Abraham was a just man who lived by faith, and his faith was manifest in many deeds. God tested him repeatedly, and Abraham consistently responded with faithful obedience. In Genesis 22, he faced the ultimate test: God commanded him to sacrifice his beloved son, Isaac. Abraham demonstrated his willingness, and he went with Isaac to Mount Moriah. But God spared Isaac and rewarded Abraham with a promise of blessing to his descendants.

Yet his descendants forfeited that blessing in the most horrific way: by fashioning a bull-calf out of gold, and then worshipping it as an idol. It was a sin of catastrophic enormity, an act of senseless ingratitude toward the God who had, quite recently and quite miraculously, delivered Israel from slavery in Egypt. By committing such a sin, the Israelites merited death.

How did Moses deliver them from the punishment they deserved? By invoking the merit of their ancestors. He told the Lord: "Remember Abraham, Isaac, and Israel, your servants, to whom you swore by yourself, and said to them, 'I will multiply your descendants as the stars of heaven, and all this land that I have promised I will give to your descendants, and they shall inherit it for ever' " (Ex 32:13).

Moses did not try to plead the cause of the current generation, except insofar as they were offspring of the great patriarchs. In this story, we can see the temporal remission of punishment. God is going to destroy the Israelites; but he doesn't. We can see Moses' intercession, based upon the treasury of merits, the merit of the Fathers.

When the ancient rabbis discussed this story, they found no other way to explain it. The treasury of merit enabled them to safeguard God's mercy and his justice simultaneously. They applied the same principles to the stories of Noah, whose righteousness served to redeem future generations from the ravages of the flood, and David, whose goodness alone saved his son Solomon from the disaster he merited for himself.

The Church Fathers understood these Old Testament stories as but dim shadows of what God the Father now does through Christ. In the Old Covenant, the merit passed from Abraham to Isaac to Israel and then to all the descendants of Israel. Now, it moves from the Father through the Son in the Spirit to Mary, the saints, the martyrs, and all of us as well.

We live in communion with others. That's true in the natural order; it's also true in the supernatural order. The saints bear our burdens, and we too must "bear one another's burdens" (Gal 6:2). St. Paul understood how this worked, and he said: "in my flesh I complete what is lacking in Christ's afflictions for the sake of his body, that is, the Church" (Col 1:24).

On the cross, Jesus pronounced, "It is finished." The perfect work of our redemption was indeed accomplished. But in another sense it was only just beginning—because, at that moment, Christ gave forth his Spirit: he empowered us, through the Holy Spirit, to share in his own life, death, and resurrection. He transferred to us everything that he had merited. And so, at the end of his earthly pilgrimage, he could say, "It is finished," and entrust his redemptive work to the Holy Spirit. The Spirit applies to the saints—and to all of us—what Christ merited through his life, death, and resurrection.

All of this is an ordered economy. It is a "managed economy," because God gave the apostles and their successors, the pope and the bishops, the power of binding and loosing (Mt 16:19, 18:18). So today we see the Church exercising the authority that Moses once exercised on Mount Sinai, the right and the duty to call upon the merits of the saints.

The Church has distributed these merits by attaching them to certain prayers, works, and sacrifices that build up Christ's body. They range from giving up smoking for a day to undertaking a pilgrimage to the Holy Land.

When the Church speaks of indulgences, it speaks of them in the context of "the full enjoyment of the benefits of the family of God" (see below). So go ahead and indulge yourself. Indulge yourself for the sake of others as well—for the living and for the dead. We're free to do so because God is at once just, merciful, and indeed indulgent. He is our Father. And he has arranged everything so that even supernatural life is a family affair.

Ponder in Your Heart

There reigns among men, by the hidden and benign mystery of the divine will, a supernatural solidarity whereby the sin of one harms the others just as the holiness of one also benefits the others. Thus the Christian faithful give each other mutual aid to attain their supernatural aim. A testimony of this solidarity is manifested in Adam himself, whose sin is passed on through propagation to all men. But of this supernatural solidarity the greatest and most perfect principle, foundation and example is Christ himself to communion with whom God has called us . . .

Following in the footsteps of Christ, the Christian faithful have always endeavored to help one another on the path leading to the heavenly Father through prayer, the exchange of spiritual goods and penitential expiation. The more they have been immersed in the fervor of charity, the more they have imitated Christ in his sufferings, carrying their crosses in expiation for their own sins and those of others, certain that they could help their brothers to obtain salvation from God the Father of mercies. This is the very ancient dogma of the Communion of the Saints, whereby the life of each individual son of God in Christ and through Christ is joined by a wonderful link to the life of all his other Christian brothers in the supernatural unity of the Mystical Body of Christ till, as it were, a single mystical person is formed.

Thus is explained the "treasury of the Church" . . . the infinite and inexhaustible value the expiation and the merits of Christ Our Lord have before God, offered as they were so that all of mankind could be set free from sin and attain communion with the Father. It is Christ the Redeemer himself in whom the satisfactions and merits of his redemption exist and find their force. This treasury also includes the truly immense, unfathomable and ever pristine value before God of the prayers and good works of the Blessed Virgin Mary and all the saints, who following in the footsteps of Christ the Lord and by his grace have sanctified their lives and fulfilled the mission entrusted to them by the Father. Thus while attaining their own salvation, they have also cooperated in the salvation of their brothers in the unity of the Mystical Body.

"For all who are in Christ, having his spirit, form one Church and cleave together in him" (Eph 4:16) . . . For this reason there certainly exists between the faithful who have already reached their heavenly home, those who are expiating their sins in purgatory and those who are still pilgrims on earth a perennial link of charity and an abundant exchange of all the goods by which, with the expiation of all the sins of the entire Mystical Body, divine justice is placated. God's mercy is thus led to forgiveness, so that sincerely repentant sinners may participate as soon as possible in the full enjoyment of the benefits of the family of God.

—Pope Paul VI, twentieth century

30.

Intercession of the Saints

The apostle Paul referred to himself as "the foremost of sinners" (I Tim I:I5). But he knew also that he was a saint.

To St. Paul, as to all the Catholic Church, all Christians are "saints" by virtue of their baptism. "Saint" means "holy one," and Christians are made holy not by anything they've learned or done, but by the indwelling of almighty God. We are holy because we are temples of the Holy Spirit—and, in Paul's worldview, nothing on earth is holier than God's Temple.

Thus, St. Paul's Letter to the Colossians begins: "To the *saints* and faithful brethren in Christ at Colossae: We always thank God, the Father of our Lord Jesus Christ, when we pray for you, because we have heard of your faith in Christ Jesus and of the love which you have for all the *saints* . . . May you be strengthened with all power, according to his glorious might, for all endurance and patience with joy, giving thanks to the Father, who has qualified us to share in the inheritance of the *saints* in light" (Col I:2–I2; italics added).

Holiness—sainthood—is simply the common Christian vocation. But, in that short passage from Colossians, Paul also distinguished between the saints on earth (Col 1:2) and the "saints in light" (Col 1:12)—what Catholic devotion would later call, respectively, the "Church militant" and the "Church triumphant." The Epistle to the Hebrews (12:1) tells us that the latter are "a cloud of witnesses" around the former.

To the saints on earth who share our calling, we give our love. To the saints in light, we give a special honor called veneration. It's not the same kind of honor we give to God alone. It is more like the profound respect we owe our parents and grandparents. We love them so much that we frame their photos and give them a prominent place in our home. We shouldn't hesitate to ask our parents for prayer; nor should we hesitate to ask our ancestors in the faith.

St. Paul himself asked for the intercession of the "saints" in Colossae (see Col 4:3). For as we share in the life and divine nature of Jesus Christ, so we share in his singular office as the "one mediator between God and men" (1 Tim 2:5). So St. Paul could "urge that supplications, prayers, intercessions, and thanksgivings be made for all men" (1 Tim 2:1). He could, moreover, promise to assure the saints in Colossae of his own intercession on their behalf: "we have not ceased to pray for you" (Col 1:9).

Knowing what we know from elsewhere in the New Testament, we can be certain that St. Paul's intercession has not ceased, even today. The book of Revelation (6:9–10) shows the martyrs in heaven, very much aware of events on earth, and crying out to God for redress. Jesus himself, in one of his parables, depicts a heavenly intercession (Lk 16:27–28).

The early Christians kept a lively devotion to the Communion of Saints. It was not simply a matter of honoring their ancestors, because they did not think of the saints as dead and therefore removed from their presence. The saints were more present to the Church on earth, because the saints lived in the presence of God. The saints were not dead; indeed, they were more alive than the Church on earth.

The devotion of the early Christians is evident in hundreds of archaeological finds, in great artworks and in semi-literate graffiti, in monuments and on common household items. The cry of the Church on earth goes up constantly to the saints in heaven: "pray for us" and "bless us."

The saints in glory were part of the great family of the Church, the anniversaries of their deaths celebrated as "birthdays" by the Christians who outlived them, and many of them observed perpetually in the calendar of the universal Church.

The scholar Peter Brown has emphasized repeatedly that this was not the superstitious devotion of the "rabble." It was not a holdover from paganism. In fact, the pagans were horrified by Christian devotion to the saints, and they condemned it as unseemly!

No, it was the greatest Scripture scholars of ancient Christianity who kept the liveliest devotion to the saints. We find it spelled out most eloquently in the writings of those biblicists we now know as St. Jerome, St. Augustine, and St. John Chrysostom.

So great was Jerome's devotion that he used to spend his Sunday afternoons strolling among the martyrs' remains in the dark corridors of the Roman catacombs.

St. John Chrysostom, in the fourth century, marveled at the role reversals created by the cult of the saints. "Even the emperor . . . who wears the purple and sets everything shaking at his nod often throws himself face down upon the martyr's tomb and calls for that saint's prayers"—a saint who, in earthly life, might have been a commoner or of no-account! Who's shaking now? He spoke also of humble wives who implored the saints' protection for their husbands who had undertaken perilous journeys.

St. Augustine preached often about the lives of the saints, and he wrote several extended defenses of Catholic devotion to the saints. He was responding mostly to attacks from the Manicheans—heretics who were so flaky that they were really more pagan than Christian. Yet their arguments are strikingly similar to those we hear from anti-Catholics today. "The prayers of the martyrs help us," he preached. "Indeed, it is through these solemnities that *your* [italics added] sanctity is commemorated . . . lest we think that we are giving something to the martyrs when we celebrate their most solemn days. They do not need our festivals. For they rejoice in heaven with the angels. They rejoice with us not so much if we honor them as if we imitate them."

Again, I hear echoes of St. Paul, who said, "Be imitators of me as I am of Christ" (1 Cor 1:11). To venerate St. Paul is to glorify Christ for his grace made manifest in the life of his family on earth. St. Paul said: "It is no longer I who live, but Christ who lives in me" (Gal 2:20). Christ indeed lives in all the saints, and he makes them even more perfectly themselves.

It is a deep fellow feeling, a family feeling, that Christians share with the saints. The fourth-century bishop St. Paulinus of Nola placed himself under the patronage of St. Felix, a martyr. In a poem he addressed the saint as "revered father, everlasting patron, Felix my nurse, Felix, dear friend of Christ."

In all the history of Christianity, so little has changed. We hear the same terms today addressed to beloved saints from down the ages: St. Jude Thaddeus, St. Francis of Assisi, St. Anthony of

Padua, St. Catherine Laboure, St. Thérèse of Lisieux, St. Maximilian Kolbe, Padre Pio.

To such figures we do not hesitate to say, "Pray for us!"

Ponder in Your Heart

It is true that Christians pay religious honor to the memory of the martyrs, both to excite us to imitate them and to gain a share in their merits and the assistance of their prayers. Yet we do not build altars to any martyr, but to the God of martyrs, although it is to the *memory* of the martyrs. No one presiding at the altar in the saints' burial place ever says, "We bring an offering to you, O Peter!" or "O Paul!" or "O Cyprian!" The offering is made to God, who gave the crown of martyrdom, while it is *in memory* [italics added] of those thus crowned.

The emotion is increased by the associations of the place, and love is excited both toward those who are our examples, and toward him by whose help we may follow such examples. We regard the martyrs with the same affectionate intimacy that we feel towards holy men of God in this life, when we know that their hearts are prepared to endure the same suffering for the truth of the Gospel. There is more devotion in our feeling toward the martyrs, because we know that their conflict is over; and we can speak with greater confidence in praise of those already victors in heaven, than of those still combating here.

What is properly divine worship, the Greeks call *latria* (for which there is no word in Latin), and both in doctrine and in practice we give this only to God. To this [divine] worship belongs the offering of sacrifices, as we see in the word *idolatry,* which means the giving of this worship to idols. Accordingly we never offer, or require anyone to offer, sacrifice to a martyr, or to a holy soul, or to any angel. Anyone falling into this error is instructed by doctrine, either in the way of correction or of caution. For holy beings themselves, whether saints or angels, refuse to accept what they know to be due to God alone. We see this in Paul and Barnabas, when the men of Lycaonia wished to sacrifice to them as gods, on account of the miracles they performed. They rent their clothes, and restrained the people, crying out to them, and persuading them that they were not gods. We see it also in the angels, as we read in the Apocalypse that an angel would not allow himself to be worshipped, and said to his worshipper, "I am your fellow-servant, and of your brethren" (Rev 19:10).

—St. Augustine of Hippo, fourth century

31.

Pilgrimage

Pilgrimage was an essential part of Jesus' religious life. The heart of ancient Judaism was the sacrificial cult of the Jerusalem Temple. There was no other temple, as there could be no other gods. As God is one, so he had only one holy city, to which he summoned his people to make pilgrimage: "Three times a year all your males shall appear before the Lord your God at the place which he will choose: at the feast of unleavened bread, at the feast of weeks, and at the feast of booths" (Dt 16:16; see also Ex 23:17). Mary and Joseph fulfilled this commandment every year. The only glimpse we have of Jesus' childhood is the story of the Holy Family's pilgrimage to Jerusalem when Jesus was twelve. He remained faithful to the obligation during his adult years, and the evangelists regularly show him going "up to Jerusalem" for the feasts (see Jn 2:13, 5:1). Even St. Paul made the required journeys, and even after his conversion: "For Paul had decided to sail past Ephesus . . . for he was hastening to be at Jerusalem, if possible, on the day of Pentecost" (Acts 20:16).

Yet the apostles foresaw a day when such pilgrimage would be obsolete. St. Paul already indicated this when he contrasted the earthly city with a heavenly one: "But the Jerusalem above is free, and she is our mother" (Gal 4:26). In the Apocalypse, St. John three times spoke of "new Jerusalem, coming down out of heaven from God" (Rev 3:12, 21:2, 21:10).

The "new Jerusalem" would not be a geographic location, but a eucharistic one. Arriving for worship, Christians had come to a new "Mount Zion and . . . city of the living God, the heavenly Jerusalem, and to innumerable angels in festal gathering, and to the assembly of the first-born who are enrolled in heaven . . . and to the spirits of just men made perfect, and to Jesus, the mediator of a new covenant, and to the sprinkled blood that speaks more graciously than the blood of Abel" (Heb 12:22–24). Heavenly Jerusalem now touched down upon earth, and it was as near as Sunday Mass.

In any event, the destruction of the Jerusalem Temple in A.D. 70 removed any question of obligatory pilgrimages. Unlike the Hebrew Scriptures and the Muslims' Koran, the Church has never required Christians to make such journeys. Yet Christians have eagerly and voluntarily taken up the practice.

The early Christians were inclined to visit the sites of Jesus' life. St. Melito of Sardis visited the sites of the passion around A.D. 170, and it exercised a profound influence upon his preaching. The ancient historian Eusebius tells us of a Cappadocian bishop who went to Jerusalem around 210 to pay homage and investigate the holy places. In the mid-fourth century, St. Helena, the mother of the emperor Constantine, made a famous Holy Land pilgrimage, during which she directed archaeological excavations.

Jerusalem retained an attractive power, because it contained the monuments of the Lord's passion. However, it was no longer the only pilgrimage destination. Pious travelers now streamed to Rome as well, to pay homage at the tombs of Saints Peter and Paul and visit the sites of their martyrdom. Pilgrims journeyed also to catch a glimpse of—and perhaps a bit of advice from—living saints. St. Anthony of Egypt developed such a reputation that he drew crowds to his desert dwelling, and many of those visitors stayed on to live near him as hermits or monks. It is said that he caused a city to appear in the midst of the wilderness.

Other destinations drew pilgrims: the sites of apparitions of Jesus or Mary . . . locations made famous in the stories of the saints . . . streams, wells, and pools reputed to have miraculous powers . . . repositories of relics . . . churches of exceptional beauty . . . and notable sacred images.

You might expect the practice of pilgrimage to be weakened by the rise of Christianity, since it was no longer an obligation, as it had been for Jews. But the practice grew stronger still. We possess many pilgrim journals and narratives, from the fourth century onward. And the subsequent centuries have only increased the ardor of Christian wanderlust (though perhaps wander*love* would be a more appropriate term).

What's even more interesting is how pilgrimage soon became the dominant metaphor for ordinary life on earth. The earliest Christians often referred to themselves as exiles and wayfarers who were homeward bound. St. Augustine portrays believers as "on pilgrimage in this condition of mortality." The magisterium has often taken up this image, speaking of the Church as the "pilgrim people of God"; and the liturgy implores the Lord to "strengthen in faith and love your pilgrim Church on earth."

A modern Catholic map of the world will offer many possible destinations for pilgrimage. Jerusalem and Rome remain favorites, but the Marian shrines at Lourdes and Fatima are also immensely popular. Since the Middle Ages, travelers have also thronged to Santiago de Compostela, the shrine of St. James in Spain. Pope John Paul II evoked the pilgrim road to Santiago as a metaphor for the life of the pilgrim Church on earth, "an example of the Church's pilgrimage on its journey towards the heavenly city." It is, he said, "a path of prayer and penance, of charity and solidarity; a stretch of the path of life where the faith, becoming history among mankind, also converts culture into something Christian. The churches and abbeys, the hospitals and shelters of the Way to Santiago still speak of the Christian adventure of making pilgrimage in which the faith becomes life, history, culture, charity and works of mercy."

Pope John Paul noted that no pilgrim—whether real or metaphorical—walks alone. We are all accompanied by the "mysterious Pilgrim of Emmaus" (see Lk 24:15–35), who opens up the Word to us and makes himself known in the breaking of the bread. All those great wonders occur whenever the heavenly Jerusalem touches down to earth, in the Holy Mass.

We need not go to the far ends of the earth to go on pilgrimage. There are humble Marian shrines within driving distance of most of our homes. Some Christians like to make small pilgrimages to nearby shrines, their diocesan cathedral, or even their own parish church, praying as they go: five decades of the Rosary along the way, five at the holy site, and five on the way back to the car. We can also make pilgrimage, as the ancients did, to visit with holy people we know, or travel to honor the graves of our ancestors and mentors.

For us, a pilgrimage is a sacramental: an outward sign of an inward grace. It reminds us that we are wayfarers as long as we live here on earth, and we must stay on the path to our glorious destination.

Ponder in Your Heart

Paula entered Jerusalem . . . And although the proconsul of Palestine, who was an intimate friend of her house, . . . gave orders to have his official residence placed at her disposal, she chose a humble cell in preference to it. Moreover, in visiting the holy places so great was the passion and the enthusiasm she exhibited for each, that she could never have torn herself away from one had she not been eager to visit the rest. Before the cross she threw herself down in adoration, as though she beheld the Lord hanging upon it: and when she entered the tomb which was the scene of the Resurrection she kissed the stone that the angel had rolled away from the door of the sepulchre. Indeed so ardent was her faith that she even licked with her mouth the very spot on which the Lord's body had lain, like one thirsty for the river that he has longed for. What tears she shed there, what groans she uttered, and what grief she poured forth, all Jerusalem knows; the Lord also to whom she prayed knows.

—St. Jerome, fourth century

32.

The Presence of God

We modern Christians have few occasions to use the word *temple.* It never caught on as a term for Christian places of worship.

In the ancient world, however, for Jews, *temple* referred to one dominant reality: it was Judaism's central sanctuary in Jerusalem, the place of worship constructed by King Solomon, destroyed and later rebuilt, and then lavishly renovated in St. Paul's lifetime by the Herodian kings. For Jews, there was only one Temple. It was the only place they were permitted to offer sacrifice; it was the divinely ordained *place of God's presence.* It was the one place on earth that could truly be called holy. It was the place where God's Spirit dwelt.

It's important for us to get this right: Jews didn't believe that God was present *only* in the Temple and *absent* from the rest of creation. They professed, as we do today, that God is everywhere. But they also held that he made himself specially present to his people in the Jerusalem Temple and its rites. The Temple was a place where they could withdraw from the pollutions of the world and know God's presence in purity.

When the Word became flesh, however, the Temple found its fulfillment in Jesus Christ, who identified *his body* as God's temple (see John 2:19–21). Somehow the form and function of the structure in Jerusalem was now taken up and perfected in Christ's flesh.

What's more, Jesus identified the temple of his body with his people, the Church (see Acts 9:4).

This revelation made a deep impression upon St. Paul, and it became a dominant theme in his preaching. The Church was now the special place of God's presence and the locus of sacrifice. "Do you not know that you are God's temple and that God's Spirit dwells in you? . . . God's temple is holy, and that temple you are" (1 Cor 3:16–17). And again: "We are the temple of the living God; as God said, 'I will live in them and move among them, and I will be their God, and they shall be my people' " (2 Cor 6:16).

No longer were God's presence and his purifying ritual confined to a single geographic location. No longer were they the exclusive privilege of a single ethnic group. Now the temple has no walls. It is universal—that is, it's *catholic.*

This line of thought continues in the Letter to the Ephesians, where we find all the creedal marks of the Church—it is one, holy, catholic, and apostolic—spelled out in terms of a temple's construction: "So then you are no longer strangers and sojourners, but you are fellow citizens with the saints and members of the household of God, built upon the foundation of the apostles and prophets, Christ Jesus himself being the cornerstone, in whom the whole structure is joined together and grows into a holy temple in the Lord; in whom you also are built into it for a *dwelling place of God in the Spirit*" (Eph 2:19–22; italics added).

Living fully in the Church, *we* are temples of God's presence. And yet Catholic tradition teaches us to "practice" God's presence and make "acts of the presence of God"—simple prayers of invocation. If God is always present in us, why do we need to make such acts?

We do it for our sake, not his! It's not as if God is a genie who requires a rub of the lamp to be conjured up. No, he's present. But we need to be reminded of that fact. And the reminder should make a difference for us.

Consider an analogy: When my beloved mother is visiting, I make a conscious effort not to indulge any verbal tics or other habits that I know will irritate her. On the other hand, I go out of my way to do and say the things that I know will please her. I do all this because I respect and love her—and maybe also because we never really lose that little child's desire to please his parents, which is a healthy species of fear and awe.

Our moms can help us with these efforts, of course. If we somehow forget they're nearby, they know how to remind us of the fact, by clearing their throat, for example, or dropping something to the floor.

How good it will be when we are so attuned to God's presence, and so keen to do what he likes and avoid what he dislikes.

Unfortunately, he doesn't often clear his throat for us. He's pleased to find other ways to keep our attention, and Catholic tradition records many of them for us. The chapters of this book can be seen, each and all, as methods of practicing God's presence.

We do it, first of all, by getting to know him better. As we study the Scriptures and spend time with the Lord in prayer, we grow deeper in our knowledge of his ways; and that is a beginning of love, because we cannot love someone we do not know.

But we can do more. We can also use more specific methods known as "prayer of the presence of God."

Prayer books offer us many formal prayers that acknowledge

God's presence. One of my favorites is the one that begins: "My Lord and my God, I firmly believe that you are here, that you see me, that you hear me. I adore you with profound reverence . . ." Of course, the first five words alone make a perfect acknowledgment, as they are the words immortalized by St. Thomas the Apostle when he recognized the risen Lord (Jn 20:28). We can also simply pray the name of Jesus, or use one of the aspirations we discussed in chapter 12.

Images, too, can help us. Perhaps our working conditions give us the freedom to keep a cross or holy card nearby. Sometimes we don't have that freedom. But we can always find a way to make reminders. I have a friend who makes a cross of two large paper clips and places it by his phone every day. Since most of his work involves the phone, he has that simple cross as a constant token of God's presence. The early Christians got around the stigma of the cross by tracing the outline of a fish in their homes and workplaces, on their lamps and loaves of bread. We can surely find our own ways to make discreet reminders.

From the various practices you encounter in this book, you'll surely encounter several that work for you. Perhaps you can work them into a plan and space them at intervals throughout the day.

We want to be aware of the presence of God at all times. Our practices of prayer and study are like vines we plant throughout the day—occasional moments of concentrated attention we pay to Our Lord. If we live them right, those moments will grow like vines and our awareness of God will cover our entire day, as ivy covers an old brick wall and makes it beautiful.

Ponder in Your Heart

In the beginning of his novitiate, [Brother Lawrence] spent the hours appointed for private prayer in thinking of God, so as to convince his mind of, and to impress deeply upon his heart, the Divine existence, rather by devout sentiments and submission to the lights of faith than by studied reasonings and elaborate meditations. By this short and sure method, he exercised himself in the knowledge and love of God, resolving to use his utmost endeavor to live in a continual sense of his presence, and, if possible, never more to forget him.

When he had thus in prayer filled his mind with great sentiments of that infinite Being, he went to his work appointed in the kitchen (for he was cook to the society); there having first considered the various things his office required, and when and how each thing was to be done, he spent all the intervals of his time, as well before as after his work, in prayer.

When he began his business, he said to God, with a son's trust in him, "O my God, since you are with me, and I must now, in obedience to your commands, apply my mind to these outward things, I beg you to grant me the grace to continue in your presence; and to this end help me with your assistance, receive all my works, and possess all my affections."

As he proceeded in his work, he continued his familiar conversation with his Maker, imploring his grace, and offering to him all his actions. When he had finished, he examined himself how he had discharged his duty; if he found well, he returned thanks to God; if otherwise, he asked pardon; and without being discouraged, he set his mind right again, and continued his exercise of the presence of God, as if he had never deviated from it. "Thus," he said, "by rising after my falls, and by frequently renewed acts of faith and love, I have come to a state, wherein it would be as difficult for me not to think of God, as it was at first to accustom myself to it."

As Brother Lawrence had found such an advantage in walking in the presence of God, it was natural for him to recommend it earnestly to others; but his example was a stronger inducement than any arguments he could propose. His facial expression was edifying; such a sweet and calm devotion appearing in it, as could not but affect the beholders. And it was observed, that in the greatest hurry of business in the kitchen, he still preserved his recollection and heavenly-mindedness. He was never hasty nor loitering, but did each thing in its season, with an even uninterrupted composure and tranquility of spirit. "The time of business," said he, "does not with me differ from the time of prayer; and in the noise and clutter of my kitchen, while several persons are at the same time calling for different things, I possess God in as great tranquility as if I were on my knees at the Blessed Sacrament."

—Anonymous recollection of
Brother Lawrence, seventeenth century

33.

ALMSGIVING

You may be asking what this topic has to do with devotions and piety. The answer is simple: it has everything to do with devotions and piety.

First of all, almsgiving flows naturally and supernaturally from our prayer. As we draw closer to Jesus, we see him as he is, and we wish to obey him; and he told his followers, in no uncertain terms, to give alms (Lk 12:33; Mt 6:2–4). What's more, as we draw closer to him, we want to be more like him; and he gave all that he had, till he had nothing left to give.

Almsgiving is *itself* a powerful form of prayer. The Good Book says: "Prayer and fasting are good, but better than either is almsgiving accompanied by righteousness . . . It is better to give alms than to store up gold; for almsgiving saves one from death and expiates every sin. Those who regularly give alms shall enjoy a full life" (Tob 12:8–9).

Why is almsgiving superior to prayer and fasting? Because it includes both and surpasses them. To give alms is to give to God.

More than raising funds for him, it's raising our mind and heart to him. It's prayer. If we're doing it right, though, it's fasting, too, because it's giving from our very substance—giving till it hurts. Jesus compared the poor widow to all the wealthy benefactors, and he found her to be the more generous: "For they all contributed out of their abundance; but she out of her poverty has put in everything she had, her whole living" (Mk 12:44).

Almsgiving derives its power from true prayer. Without prayer, it easily degenerates into mere philanthropy: a smiling photo op and boost for our pride.

Heartfelt prayer, on the other hand, will always lead us to more generous giving. This is especially true of our participation in the Mass. The more devout we are, the more we should be sensing the call to give of ourselves, to give from our substance. The earliest Christians knew this: we cannot make a good Communion if we are neglecting the poor. Consider the words of St. John Chrysostom, writing in the fourth century: "Do you wish to honor the body of Christ? Do not ignore him when he is naked. Do not pay him homage in the temple clad in silk, only then to neglect him outside where he is cold and ill-clad. He who said: 'This is my body' is the same who said: 'You saw me hungry and you gave me no food,' and 'Whatever you did to the least of my brothers you did also to me' . . . What good is it if the eucharistic table is overloaded with golden chalices when your brother is dying of hunger? Start by satisfying his hunger and then with what is left you may adorn the altar as well."

Much earlier than that, around the year A.D. 107, St. Ignatius of Antioch made the same connection. In fact, he noted that the twin marks of heresy are the neglect of the poor and neglect of the Eucharist: "They have no care for charity, none for the widow, none for the orphan, none for the afflicted, none for the prisoner, none for the hungry or the thirsty. They abstain from the Eucharist and (the common) prayer because they confess not that the Eucharist is the Flesh of our Savior Jesus Christ."

And lest we think that the demands of the Christian life have changed since then, we should heed the example of Catholics who are closer to us. Some of them live in your parish, and they're probably running the local Meals on Wheels program—but you see them first at daily Mass.

They all give heroically, and sometimes their work gets noticed. Dorothy Day, the founder of the Catholic Worker Movement, exemplified this eucharistic almsgiving to a very high degree. Robert Ellsberg said of her: "She believed in the real presence of Christ in the consecrated bread and wine on the altar. But she believed that Christ was also truly present in the poor. And so our response to the poor was a test of the authenticity of our worship. How could we love God whom we haven't seen if we haven't loved our neighbor whom we have seen? And how could we love our neighbors who are hungry except by feeding them? The mystery of the poor is this: that they are Jesus and what you do for them you do to him."

The Eucharist is the key to a civilization of love. It saves us from misguided tenderness and feel-good philanthropy, because it gives us the grace to sacrifice as Jesus did. It gives us the very grace of Jesus' sacrifice. The Eucharist saves us, too, from falling into a messiah complex, since through Holy Communion we let the true Messiah work through us.

The phenomenon has been observed and documented by non-Catholics. The Anglican scholar Gregory Dix said it was "a matter of observable historical fact" that "a 'high' doctrine of the sacrament has always been accompanied by an aroused conscience as to the condition of Christ's poor."

Still more recently, the sociologist Robert Bellah, an Episcopalian, noted that Roman Catholic eucharistic piety is the last great hope for American society. "The cultural code that we need to change is deeper," he said, "than ideology or policy analysis; it is rooted in . . . the religious imagination . . . I believe we need at this moment to reconstitute our cultural code by giving much greater salience to the sacramental life . . . and, in particular, to the Eucharist . . . It is in that moment that we become members one of another, that we not only partake of the Eucharist but can actually become Eucharist, ourselves completing 'what is lacking in Christ's afflictions,' as St. Paul says in Colossians, by self-giving love for the whole world."

Pope Paul VI once asked: "Do you want peace?" Then, assuming the affirmative, he answered: "Work for justice." In turn, we might ask ourselves: "Do we want justice?" The answer for us, as for the early Christians, is an altar call. I quote the passage in another chapter, but it bears repeating. That's why it has survived since at least the third century: "Widows and orphans are to be revered like the altar of sacrifice."

This leaves all kinds of practical questions. For example, how much should we give? Some people scrupulously tithe—that is, they give a tenth of their before-tax income to charities. That's laudable. It's not divinely revealed, however; and for some people, in some years, that may not be enough. When others have greater need, we must respond with greater giving. Yet at other times, we may not have even that tenth to give away.

So we find ourselves back where we started: at prayer, at the altar. If we can look at our eucharistic Lord—who gives himself to us, holding nothing back—and honestly tell him that we're giving as much as we can, then we're probably giving as much as we should. If not, it's probably time to reexamine our giving.

Ponder in Your Heart

Christ understood that we have a terrible hunger for God . . . that we have been created to be loved, and so he made himself a Bread of Life and he said, "Unless you eat my flesh and drink my blood, you cannot live, you cannot love, you cannot serve" . . .

He also wants to give us the chance to put our love for him in living action. He makes himself the hungry one, not only for bread, but for love. He makes himself the naked one, not only for a piece of cloth but for that understanding love, that dignity, human dignity. He makes himself the homeless one, not only for the piece of a small room, but for that deep sincere love for the other. And this is the Eucharist. This is Jesus, the Living Bread that he has come to break with you and me.

—Blessed Mother Teresa of Calcutta,
twentieth century

VIII

Love of My Life

34.

Devotion to the Trinity

We Christians tend to treat the Trinity as a punctuation mark. We invoke the Holy Name when we make the Sign of the Cross at the beginning of our prayer. Maybe we end our prayer the same way, or with a Glory Be, which is a Trinitarian prayer. But, in between, we don't spend much time puzzling over the one God who is three persons. Who can blame us? It is a mystery too deep for anyone to plumb, so why bother troubling ourselves over it?

I'm reminded of the catechism teacher who asked her class to define *mystery.* A little boy raised his hand and said: "Oh, that's something we have to believe, even though we know it's not true."

While we can surely sympathize with the boy's bafflement, we're obliged to dissent from his concluding judgment. For we know that the mystery of the Trinity is true. In fact, it's the truest thing we can know. Far more than a punctuation mark at the beginning and end of our prayer, the Trinity is rather the sum, substance, subject, and object of our prayer. Consider what the *Catechism of the Catholic Church* has to say about the Trinity.

> The mystery of the Most Holy Trinity is the central mystery of Christian faith and life. It is the mystery of God in himself. It is therefore the source of all the other mysteries of faith, the light that enlightens them. It is the most fundamental and essential teaching in the "hierarchy of the truths of faith." The whole history of salvation is identical with the history of the way and the means by which the one true God, Father, Son, and Holy Spirit, reveals himself to men "and reconciles and unites with himself those who turn away from sin." (CCC, n. 234)

The Trinity is the reason for every season, the central reality of every feast of the Church, the source of all the other mysteries and all the other devotions. All the sacraments and all Catholic liturgy are *about* the Blessed Trinity.

So why do we gingerly step around it, or hurry through it as a formality?

Our basic problem, I believe, is in the way we think about "mystery." We tend to consider mysteries in almost mathematical terms: they are problems so enigmatic, so contradictory that they cannot ever be solved. The doctrine of the Trinity does present us with a seeming contradiction. It tells us that three equals one when we know that three doesn't equal one. Yet we have to believe it or forfeit the name *Christian,* so we assent and we move on to the prayer at hand.

But mystery is not mathematics. It would be more helpful for us to think of mystery in terms of marriage, or indeed any deep human relationship. We cannot ever "figure out" a spouse, but we can certainly grow in love, knowledge, and understanding of that person.

The Trinity is the loving relationship we hope to know forever in heaven. If we are not growing in our love of that mystery, we are not growing any closer to heaven. And, if that's so, then our faith is superficial. We're missing the point of the "whole history of salvation," which is identical with the revelation of the Trinitarian God.

God the Father sent the Son so that we might receive the Spirit. Why is that? Remember: God became what we are, so that we might become what he is. He assumed our nature, so that we might share in his. Heaven is nothing other than that sharing, that communion, and it has begun already, with our baptism.

The word *Trinity* does not appear in the Scriptures. It is a theological term coined by Christians to describe the reality at the heart of divine revelation. St. Matthew's Gospel ends with Jesus' command for the disciples to baptize "in the name of the Father and of the Son and of the Holy Spirit" (Mt 28:19). It is an enigmatic phrase as it speaks of one "name," but then actually *names* three persons. St. Paul assumes this same mystery when he pronounces the benediction that we use in the Mass: "The grace of the Lord Jesus Christ and the love of God and the fellowship of the Holy Spirit be with you all" (2 Cor 13:14).

Indeed, for St. Paul, every aspect of Christian religion is a Trinitarian mystery. Consider prayer. Paul begins from a premise that is confirmed by experience, at least in my case: "for we do not know how to pray as we ought" (Rom 8:26). It's a real problem: we wish to speak with a God who is wholly other than we are. How do we find a common language? Where do we begin?

We have a common language because God has given us his eternal Word. We pray from within Christ, and we pray with the power of his Spirit. In fact, "the Spirit himself intercedes for us with sighs too deep for words" (Rom 8:26). Christian prayer is itself a proof of the life we have come to share through baptism: "it is the

Spirit himself bearing witness with our spirit that we are children of God" (Rom 8:16). For St. Paul we are now living "in Christ" (Rom 8:1), and so we can speak to the Father, in all truth, with the Spirit of the Son. We can call him "*Abba!* Father!" and mean it, and speak the truth.

We have been taken up into the life of the Trinity, even now. We do not have to wait to live in heaven. Heaven has come to us—though we still await the day of consummation, when we shall be like him, for we shall see him as he is (see 1 Jn 3:2). All prayer, then, is Trinitarian, and not just in its punctuation.

For St. Paul, all morality, too, is Trinitarian, as our every action should express our communion with God. In fact, a Christian consideration of *any* religious matter should find its grounding in the Trinity, though that ground may often be assumed and unspoken.

In prayer, however, we speak it all the time, and not only in the Sign of the Cross and the Glory Be.

At Mass, so many of the prayers should remind us of the mystery. The Mass itself is a Trinitarian prayer: Worshipping in the Spirit, we unite ourselves with the Son as he offers himself to the Father. We make the Sign of the Cross and pronounce St. Paul's benediction. We pray our prayers in threes: the Kyrie, for example, and the Sanctus, the "thrice-holy hymn." We don't repeat "have mercy" and "holy" merely for emphasis. We are implicitly invoking the Trinity. And we do so *explicitly* in other Mass prayers, such as the Gloria and the Nicene Creed.

Our Christian vocation is Trinitarian. The Trinity is the mystery at the heart of our faith, and God wants us to place it at the heart of our lives. Yet he is so unlike us that it is hard for us even to begin to contemplate his inner life. It helps, of course, that he has become man for our sake.

But how else can we go deeper into the mystery? Pope John

Paul II proposed that we should begin by considering a relationship we know very well: the mystery of family life. For "*the primordial model of the family is to be sought in God himself*, in the Trinitarian mystery of his life. The divine 'We' is the eternal pattern of the human 'we,' especially of that 'we' formed by the man and the woman created in the divine image and likeness." The same pope put the matter still more concisely when he said: "God in his deepest mystery is not a solitude but a family, since he has in himself fatherhood, sonship, and the essence of family, which is love." Perhaps we will begin to know God, the eternal divine family, when we prayerfully consider what an earthly family should be.

We are created for the sake of love. When we experience love in family life, it is heavenly, but it is still only an image of the greater glory we will behold in heaven, a glory we proclaim even now: Glory be to the Father and to the Son and to the Holy Spirit: as it was in the beginning, is now, and ever shall be, world without end. Amen!

Ponder in Your Heart

To us ignorant people it appears that all three Persons of the Blessed Trinity are—as represented in paintings—in one person, as when three faces are painted on one body. And thus we are so scared away that it seems the mystery is impossible and that no one should desire to think about it. For the intellect feels hindered and fears lest it might have doubts about this truth, and it thereby loses something very beneficial.

What was represented to me [in a vision] were three distinct persons, for we can behold and speak to each one. Afterward I reflected that only the Son took human flesh, through which this truth of the Trinity was seen. These persons love, communicate with, and know each other . . . And this is a very great truth for which I would die a thousand deaths. In all three persons there is no more than one will, one power, and one dominion, in such a way that one cannot do anything without the others.

—St. Teresa of Avila, sixteenth century

35.

The Rosary

"For behold, henceforth all generations will call me blessed" (Lk 1:48).

Every time we pray the Rosary, we fulfill that prophecy at least fifty times. We call the Virgin Mary "blessed," using the inspired words of Holy Writ. We address her with the greeting of the angel Gabriel: "Hail, full of grace, the Lord is with you" (Lk 1:28). We proclaim her privileges, using the words of Elizabeth her kinswoman: "Blessed are you among women, and blessed is the fruit of your womb!" (Lk 1:42). To repeat these words is a delight, because they're rich with meaning, amplified by the Gospel scenes that are the focus of our meditations.

The Rosary is a time-proven method of meditative prayer. For centuries the popes have recommended it, the saints have prayed it daily. It is beloved by laborers, by children, by busy commuters, and by scientific geniuses. It was the favorite prayer of the great biologist Louis Pasteur.

Praying the Rosary, we repeat certain prayers as we ponder certain events ("mysteries") in the lives of Jesus and Mary, and we count our repetitions using beads strung together in groups of ten. Yet, like so many other devotions, the Rosary is a form that allows for variation. The Rosary of the "Seven Sorrows," for example, includes seven groups of seven beads. Some people end their Rosary with a "Hail, Holy Queen," others with the Litany of Loreto, and still others with a series of prayers for the pope. Some even conclude their Marian marathon with all of the above! There are ethnic varieties as well: pious Germans, for instance, have the custom of improvising a mystery-specific insertion for each Hail Mary. For example, while meditating on the Annunciation, they pray, "Blessed is the fruit of your womb, Jesus . . . the Word who became flesh." While meditating on the Crucifixion, they might pray, "Blessed is the fruit of your womb, Jesus . . . who died for our sins."

The Church has officially recognized twenty "mysteries" appropriate for meditation. We should find them all in Scripture, in order to meditate on them more fruitfully: the five Joyful Mysteries (the Annunciation, the Visitation, the Nativity, the Presentation, and the Finding in the Temple); the five Luminous Mysteries (the Baptism of Our Lord, the Wedding Feast at Cana, the Proclamation of the Kingdom, the Transfiguration, and the Institution of the Eucharist at the Last Supper); the five Sorrowful Mysteries (the Agony in the Garden, the Scourging, the Crowning with Thorns, the Carrying of the Cross, and the Crucifixion); and the five Glorious Mysteries (the Resurrection, the Ascension, the Descent of the Holy Spirit, the Assumption, and the Coronation of Our Lady). Pope John Paul II suggested that each set of mysteries be assigned to certain days of the week: Joyful on Mondays and Saturdays, Luminous on Thursdays, Sorrowful on Tuesdays and Fridays,

Glorious on Wednesdays and Sundays. There are other, "unofficial" sets of mysteries in circulation, too, the products of occasional groundswells of scriptural and Marian piety. Through the years I've seen many—the Eucharistic Mysteries, for example, the Healing Mysteries, and the Mysteries of the Church. I never saw a set I didn't like, though for my own prayer I'm partial to the basic twenty.

The Rosary *works*, on a human level, because it engages the whole person. It involves our speech and our hearing. It occupies our mind and incites our emotions. It assigns a task to our fingertips, those sensitive organs of touch. If we pray before a sacred image, we feed our meditation through yet another bodily sense. This is how the risen Lord confirms the faith of his disciples: "See my hands and my feet, that it is I myself; handle me, and see" (Lk 24:39). It is not enough for us merely to hear him—never mind only read his words. We want him to fill up our senses.

And he does, thanks to the love of his mother. In the Scriptures, she appears as the first disciple. When gentiles come from far away in search of Jesus, they find "the child with Mary his mother" (Mt 2:11). When she sees people in need, she intercedes for them (Jn 2:3). When Jesus dies on the cross, abandoned by his friends, she remains with him; and Jesus gives her to his "beloved disciple" (that means you and me), saying, "Behold, your mother" (Jn 19:27). Thus, she helps us to meditate in a way that she uniquely can. She helps us as his mother—and so, an eyewitness of his whole life. But she helps us also as our mother, given to us by Jesus, loving us as only a mother can.

With Mary we watch the events of our salvation as they unfold. We give ourselves to the Rosary as a multisensory experience. People get hung up when they try too hard to master the various elements as individual tasks: saying the prayers, fingering the beads, and thinking very hard about the Gospel scenes with excruciatingly exact historical verisimilitude.

No. The Rosary works best when we stop working—when we stop multitasking and abandon ourselves like children to the time we're spending with our mother. The best way to get ourselves to relax is by praying the Rosary itself! In the years just before his election as Pope Benedict XVI, Cardinal Joseph Ratzinger told an interviewer: "repetition is a way of settling oneself into the rhythm of tranquility. It's not so much a matter of consciously concentrating on the meaning of each single word, but allowing myself on the contrary to be carried away by the calm of repetition and of steady rhythm. So much the more so, since this text does not lack content. It brings great images and visions and above all the figure of Mary—and then, through her, the figure of Jesus—before my eyes and in my soul."

There is nothing vain about such repetition. To pray in this way is to please Our Lord, who told his disciples, "And in praying do not heap up empty phrases as the Gentiles do" (Mt 6:7). True Christians, on the contrary, never tire of repeating the Rosary's prayers, which are phrases of fulfillment.

The best place to pray the Rosary is with the family. When Father Patrick Peyton said, "The family that prays together stays together," he was talking about the Rosary. Pope John Paul II was a tireless promoter of the family Rosary, and even coined a title for the Blessed Virgin, "Queen of the Family," which he attached to the end of the most popular Marian litany. All these initiatives surely pleased Our Lady. After Mother Teresa of Calcutta endured a harrowing vision of Calvary, she recorded that Mary reassured her: "Fear not. Teach them to say the Rosary—the family Rosary—and all will be well."

It is difficult to make the family Rosary fit the schedule of a busy household. There was a time in my family when we found it almost impossible to trap all our sports-minded teenagers in the house at once. So we did what we could. We locked onto the one time when we were almost always together—dinner—and we concluded our meal with a decade. This served as our "down payment" on the family Rosary till we could do a better job of taming our schedules.

Though the family Rosary is a powerful grace, the experience of the Rosary is a very individual thing. People differ in their capacity for certain prayers, as we differ in everything else. It's true even of popes. Pope John Paul II was known to pray many decades of the Rosary every day. Pope Benedict has confessed that sometimes the intensity of three decades of meditation is overwhelming, and he has to pause the devotion.

Not all of us will experience the Rosary with such emotion. Some of us have a hard enough time keeping focus—even with all our senses engaged.

Nevertheless, it would be sinful pride to abandon such a prayer simply because we don't pray it well. When my children were very small, they would often present me with "artworks" that were really no more than smudges and scribbles. But to me they were masterpieces—and more: they were sacraments of love. My life would have been impoverished if any of my children had abandoned the practice because, at age four, they could not paint the *Mona Lisa.*

To God and to the Blessed Virgin, all our efforts at prayer are precious. When we persevere in praying the Rosary, we become like little children (see Mt 18:3), children of Mary, children of our heavenly Father.

Blessed Pope John XXIII, a childlike son of Mary, had excellent advice for those who grew frustrated with their own inattention as they tried to pray the Rosary. Such people gave up, with the excuse that they'd rather pray no Rosary than a bad one. He corrected them, saying that a "bad Rosary" is one left unsaid.

Ponder in Your Heart

The Rosary, though clearly Marian in character, is at heart a Christocentric prayer. In the sobriety of its elements, it has *all the depth of the Gospel message in its entirety,* of which it can be said to be a compendium. It is an echo of the prayer of Mary, her perennial *Magnificat* for the work of the redemptive incarnation which began in her virginal womb. With the Rosary, the Christian people *sits at the school of Mary* and is led to contemplate the beauty on the face of Christ and to experience the depths of his love. Through the Rosary the faithful receive abundant grace, as though from the very hands of the mother of the Redeemer.

—Pope John Paul II, twentieth century

36.

Scapulars and Medals

Medals have been part of Catholic life since the early centuries of the Church. Archaeologists have turned up countless examples of such personal ornaments, the most popular being the cross. Some are free-standing, some are inscribed on a medallion. Medals of the Blessed Virgin Mary have always been popular, and museums have examples dating back to antiquity. The saints, too, have adorned the bodies of believers since way back. The early Church in Egypt was especially devoted to St. Menas, whose grave was at a spring renowned for its healing waters. St. Menas's image has turned up on pilgrim tokens as far away as France!

Through the centuries, the faithful have worn their devotion to many more saints. Browse the displays of any Catholic religious-goods store, and you can sometimes tell the saints' popularity by the number of medals that bear their likeness. Some are constants: St. Joseph, St. Jude, St. Benedict, St. Christopher, St. Thérèse, Padre Pio.

We wear scapulars, too. Scapulars are cloth items usually worn over the shoulders; and, like medals, they come in many varieties. So many, in fact, that we could write a book exclusively about scapulars and medals. Instead, however, I'd like to consider, in an exemplary way, the one I wear—the brown scapular of Our Lady—since it is, by far, the most commonly worn. And, besides, it's the one I've thought about the most!

A scapular is a sign of a commitment to the contemplative life. It originated as part of a monk's habit—the distinctive clothing he wears that sets him apart from other people. The scapular was, in the ancient world, a large overgarment that protected the monk's tunic while he was working. It was usually made of wool, and it was meant to stretch across the shoulders and down the front of the tunic, so that it looked almost cruciform. The word scapular comes from the Latin word for shoulder, *scapula.* Over time, the *scapular* became the most distinctive and characteristic form of a monk's clothing.

Over time, too, laypeople sought ways to share in the benefits of monastic life. We may not live cloistered behind monastery walls, but we long to be contemplatives in the middle of the world. So we take certain practices of prayer and meditation, and we modify them to our workaday lives. Some people pray the monastic "hours" of prayer, for example.

The small scapular is a sign of our share in the consecrated lives of monks and nuns. It's not as large as a full scapular. Specifically, the brown scapular is the way I share in the merits and good works of the Carmelite order.

The brown scapular consists of two small squares of brown cloth, one worn on the chest and the other on the back, joined by two strings or ribbons. When I decided to wear a scapular, I asked a priest to bless the item and "invest" me with it, using prayers that are approved for that purpose. In investing me with the scapular,

Father enrolled me in the Carmelite order (though the wearing of a scapular requires no vows, personal consecration, or lifetime commitments). Any priest or deacon may perform this ceremony.

From the start I was aware of the deep biblical roots of this practice. The Carmelite order traces its origins back to the Old Testament prophets Elijah and Elisha, who lived reclusive lives on remote Mount Carmel, in the hill country of Samaria (see 1 Kgs 18:19 and 2 Kgs 2:25, 4:25). The brown scapular itself evokes the "mantle of Elijah" that Elisha took up and wore as his own (see 2 Kgs 12:14).

The last of the prophets, St. John the Baptist, also wore poor and distinctive clothing—coarse garments made of camel hair (Mt 3:4)—and he lived as a desert recluse. He went, therefore, in the "spirit and power of Elijah" (Lk 1:17), and Jesus explicitly identified John with Elijah (Mk 9:13).

Christians of old read those Scriptures and longed to live like the prophets. Some discerned the call to make pilgrimage to the Holy Land and live as hermits on Mount Carmel. That was the beginning of the Carmelite order.

My share in that life is not so exotic or heroic. In fact, it's hidden—hidden in the traffic I merge with on the highway, hidden in the office I inhabit for hours every day, hidden amid the children who gather around my table every evening. It's hidden like the brown scapular I wear beneath my shirt. But it's no less real. My scapular reminds me, in all those circumstances, that I am joined with a *spiritual family* with members dispersed throughout the earth and throughout the centuries—a family whose members share certain ideals and customs.

The Carmelite order has always cultivated a particular and intense devotion to the Blessed Virgin Mary, and it is her image that usually appears on the brown scapular. It's said that, in the thirteenth century, she appeared to a Carmelite named St. Simon Stock (so named because he lived in the trunk of a tree!), and she told him that those who died "clothed in this habit will never suffer eternal fire."

Pope John Paul II said that the scapular is powerful precisely because it is a "habit" in every sense of the word, both a uniform and a pattern of good belief and good behavior. If we are faithful to the wearing of the scapular, we will be faithful to the life of Carmel—of Elijah and Elisha and John, of Jesus and Mary.

When I put the scapular back on every day, after I step out of the shower, I am deliberately taking on a life, refreshing my will to live a lifestyle that's heavenly even now. How could it fail to lead me to heaven in the end? It's no wonder that so many people kiss the scapular as they don it every day.

St. Thérèse of Lisieux said: "How happy I am that you are clothed in the holy scapular! It is a sure sign of predestination, and besides are you not more intimately united by means of it to your little sisters in Carmel?"

Again, there are many scapulars beside the brown scapular. The Benedictines have custody of one, the Dominicans another, the Norbertines still another. Since 1910, Catholics have been permitted to wear a scapular medal in place of a cloth scapular, and many people do. The scapular medal bears the image of Jesus' Sacred Heart on one side, and the image of Mary on the other.

Ponder in Your Heart

The sign of the scapular points to an effective synthesis of Marian spirituality, which nourishes the devotion of believers and makes them sensitive to the Virgin

Mother's loving presence in their lives. The scapular is essentially a "habit." Those who receive it are associated more or less closely with the Order of Carmel and dedicate themselves to the service of Our Lady for the good of the whole Church. Those who wear the scapular are thus brought into the land of Carmel, so that they may "eat its fruits and its good things" (cf. Jer 2:7), and experience the loving and motherly presence of Mary in their daily commitment to be clothed in Jesus Christ and to manifest him in their life for the good of the Church and the whole of humanity.

Therefore two truths are evoked by the sign of the scapular: on the one hand, the constant protection of the Blessed Virgin, not only on life's journey, but also at the moment of passing into the fullness of eternal glory; on the other, the awareness that devotion to her cannot be limited to prayers and tributes in her honor on certain occasions, but must become a "habit," that is, a permanent orientation of one's own Christian conduct, woven of prayer and interior life, through frequent reception of the sacraments and the concrete practice of the spiritual and corporal works of mercy. In this way the scapular becomes a sign of the "covenant" and reciprocal communion between Mary and the faithful: indeed, it concretely translates the gift of his mother, which Jesus gave on the cross to John and, through him, to all of us, and the entrustment of the beloved Apostle and of us to her, who became our spiritual Mother.

—Pope John Paul II, twentieth century

37.

Mental Prayer

I sometimes wonder if many Catholics are put off by mental prayer just because the name is so intimidating and esoteric. It conjures up images of a guy with eyes closed and fingers on his temples, moving objects that are twenty feet across the room.

But it's actually something more humble and homey. St. Teresa of Avila summed it up as "nothing else than a close sharing between friends; it means taking time frequently to be alone with him who we know loves us."

There is a sense in which all prayer is "mental prayer," because our minds should be fully engaged by the other prayers we do: the Mass, the Rosary, novenas, and so on. St. John of Damascus defined prayer itself as "the raising of the mind to God."

There is, however, a sort of prayer that emphasizes our mental faculties above all others, raising the mind to God in quiet, intimate conversation. And this is what Christian tradition calls mental prayer.

We acquire the "mind of Christ" (I Cor 2:16) by spending

time in his company, in quiet, intimate conversation. We know this by experience. We have all been influenced by our friends, our teachers, our parents; and we know that the influence is generally greater, the more time we spend with a person in quiet, intimate conversation.

Over time we learn, however, that quiet conversation is something that doesn't just happen, at least not very often. Life is busy, life is noisy, and a sustained conversation sometimes requires planning and care.

Sustaining a conversation with God does, too. Just as in a marriage or friendship, such conversation is necessary for intimacy.

We need to set time aside for mental prayer. Are you too busy for a half hour? St. Francis de Sales said that if we're too busy to pray for a half hour, then we need to pray for an hour! Many spiritual writers set twenty minutes a day as an absolute minimum. It takes several minutes just to warm up the conversation. We should also spend some time in a receptive attitude, "listening" for God's word in our soul.

It's good for us to find a time and place where we can do it well. Some people are at their best early in the morning, before the day's distractions set in. Others don't feel quite human till later in the day. Only you will know what time is best for your conversation with God.

The best place is before the tabernacle in a church. But, if we can't get there, we should at least strive to find someplace quiet, with few distractions. (Turn off your cell phone.)

It's best to begin by making an "act of the presence of God," a short prayer addressing God and acknowledging his presence: "My Lord and my God, I firmly believe that you are here, that you see me, that you hear me." This is how we "look him in the eye," so to speak. It makes the rest of the conversation flow more easily.

What should we talk to him about? Everything is fair game. About our day. Our friends. Our family members—children, parents, spouse. Consider them one by one, and raise your concerns to him. Ask good things for them. Ask what you might do to serve them better. Our mental prayer shouldn't be the time we merely rattle off intentions to God. But we do need to take our concerns to our prayer, and talk to him about them.

We also need to learn to sit back and listen. This will take faith, and a conscious effort, receiving God's word into our souls, knowing that we might not even be aware that it is happening. Our soul doesn't operate with the same sort of consciousness as our senses and our brain. We might not perceive that we are receiving God's response, but we can be sure that we are. It could be years before we recognize what happened, in prayer, at a given point in our lives.

There are obstacles and difficulties in mental prayer. We will often have to overcome distractions, for example. Yet we need not be discouraged by them. The things that distract us can become the stuff of our prayer. They may be our real concerns, after all, the things we can't seem to shake off when we leave the office or home. We should refer them to Our Lord, and ask him for light.

Sometimes, though, we may be distracted by things that shouldn't be our concerns: impure thoughts or memories, for example. But, again, if we call on God's help and persevere, we will win many graces in the struggle. The Blessed Virgin Mary can be a great help. She wants us to succeed.

If we find ourselves in a time of dryness, with nothing to say to Our Lord, we can speak to him about that, too, and ask him what he's going to do about it. We can also bring along the Bible or a spiritual book and just use its lines as a springboard for prayer, referring each line to God for light. St. Teresa did this through a period of dryness that lasted more than a decade.

Or, if we feel so moved and we don't feel the need for words, we can practice mental prayer the way one of St. John Vianney's parishioners did. He sat before the tabernacle, he explained, saying "I look at him and he looks at me."

In a sense, we need to turn all our prayer into mental prayer, even our singing of hymns! St. Paul said: "What am I to do? I will pray with the spirit and I will pray with the mind also; I will sing with the spirit and I will sing with the mind also" (1 Cor 14:15). We also need to set aside time every day for conversation with God. Never mind the name, it's nothing exotic or esoteric—just elemental, fundamental, mental prayer.

Ponder in Your Heart

Mental prayer consists of . . . being aware and knowing that we are speaking, with whom we are speaking, and who we ourselves are who dare to speak so much with so great a Lord. To think about this and other similar things, of how little we have served him and how much we are obliged to serve him, is mental prayer. Don't think it amounts to some other kind of gibberish, and don't let the name frighten you.

To recite the Our Father or the Hail Mary or whatever prayer you wish is vocal prayer. But behold what poor music you produce when you do this without mental prayer.

—St. Teresa of Avila, sixteenth century

38.

Reverence for the Tabernacle

There are certain gestures that mark us off as Catholics, and the genuflection is certainly one of them. That brief bending of one knee is rarely used in everyday life. Yet for Catholics it's an instinctive motion. It can be almost Pavlovian. I once saw a group of seminarians enter a movie theatre, and several of them dutifully genuflected—and then promptly blushed—before entering their row of seats.

Surely God will forgive them the excesses of a good habit. In their bones and nerves and muscle memory, they know a profound truth: "And the Word became flesh and dwelt among us, full of grace and truth; we have beheld his glory, glory as of the only Son from the Father" (Jn 1:14). The Greek text of the Gospel tells us that the divine Word "tabernacled" among us. He pitched his tent here.

The early Christians delighted in that fact, just as that group of seminarians did, so many years later. Once the priest had pronounced the words of consecration over the elements of bread and wine, they were changed completely and abidingly into the body and blood of Jesus Christ. To say that the presence was merely symbolic would be infidelity. To say that it lasted only as long as the liturgy would be heresy. St. Justin Martyr, living in Rome around A.D. 150, witnessed to Jesus' permanent presence in the Eucharist. He spoke of the deacons taking the sacrament to the sick and homebound, after the Mass had ended. Tertullian, writing a generation later in North Africa, related that, in times of persecution, Christians reserved the sacrament in their home, showing it the utmost reverence. Soon after that, Hippolytus of Rome wrote of the need to keep the Eucharist in a solid, impenetrable box.

Thus, reservation and reverence were hallmarks of the Church's eucharistic practice, from the earliest years and in lands as far flung as Rome and North Africa. Once Christianity was legalized, the Church Fathers left even more records. We learn, for example, that St. Basil (in the mid-fourth century) used a dove-shaped tabernacle, suspended above his church's altar. A few years later, St. Paulinus of Nola, in Italy, described something more like the tabernacles we know today: an alcove built into his newly constructed church.

They knew it then, as we know it today: Jesus is really present in the Blessed Sacrament—body, blood, soul, and divinity. That presence is lasting. And if it is lasting it should be acknowledged. He must be worshipped. For it is written, "As I live, says the Lord, every knee shall bow to me" (Rom 14:11). If, as St. Paul says, "at the *name* [italics added] of Jesus every knee should bow, in heaven and on earth and under the earth" (Phil 2:10), how much more before his bodily presence!

Nowadays, our churches keep their consecrated eucharistic hosts in a structure called a tabernacle. The name evokes John 1:14 and also the portable tent of God's presence employed by the ancient Israelites. According to Church law, a tabernacle should be "immovable, made of solid or opaque material, and locked so that the danger of profanation may be entirely avoided." The tabernacle should be in "a place that is conspicuous, suitably adorned and conducive to prayer." It is clear that the Church intends the tabernacle to be a place of divine worship.

So we do what is expected of us. Any time we pass a tabernacle, we make a brief bend of the right knee. We can do more, too, and we should. Apart from our regular attendance at Mass, we can drop by the church and make a short "visit" to Jesus in the Blessed Sacrament. It can be a great teaching moment if we take young people with us. It's a powerful, tacit way to teach the doctrine of the real presence—and it speaks more eloquently and memorably than a hundred catechisms. The visit needn't be long, just a few minutes to greet Jesus and offer a silent prayer.

Catholics also honor the altars in our churches. When we pass them, we stop and make a small bow of the head or from the waist. We learn altar piety from Jesus, who assumed a great reverence for the altar of the Jerusalem Temple (see Mt 23:19–20), but also from the Church Fathers, who managed to create a civilization of love, emanating from their sanctuaries. "Widows and orphans are to be revered as the altar of sacrifice."

Our charity is an expression of our eucharistic faith and life. It presupposes our reverence for Christ's body—a reverence that begins before the tabernacle and the altar, but goes with us wherever we travel. Even to the movie theater.

Ponder in Your Heart

My mother used to take me for walks, but she did not walk past churches. Churches were for going into. She a truth of faith to a very small child. But it was a child who, in Baptism, had received the great gift of faith. Even then, without my knowing it, the Lord had given my small mind a preparedness to grasp as true the good things he wanted me to know. Now I knew one of the best things.

—Ronald Lawler, O.F.M. Cap., twentieth century

took me in, guided me all the way to tl
rail, and knelt to pray.

I saw the earnestness with which her li
etly, and felt the attention with which s
one I certainly could not see nor hear. He
was in her prayer. Obviously she was talk
one important, though all I could see
tabernacle and the flickering light near it.

All this fascinated me, but not for lo
short time, I had had enough. I pulled o
"Time to go." She seemed not even to he
said the same thing over and over, my voic
getting louder and louder.

Finally we left. As we left, my mother
"That is where Jesus is." From the time I was
fant, I am sure, before I understood anyt
through times when my understanding was m
she had spoken to me of Jesus, our Savior and

Now if my mother said Jesus was right here
was very wise), and if Jesus said so himself: w
was it. Catholic faith in the Eucharist had be
claimed to me, and I knew it was true.

Later, when I did graduate work in psycho
could spell out reasons why a child can feel sure
the most astonishing things said by a parent. Bu
in theology I studied the nature and causes of
could see why even as a child my faith was not
subjective "feeling sure," that might just disa
when more sophisticated wondering about the
began.

In this wonderful and fearful world, in which
really dwells, someone who had divine faith had sp

IX

Life Goes On

39.

Preparation for Death

There is a sense in which "care for the dying" is what we do all the time. For we "know neither the day nor the hour" (Mt 25:13). I've taught very young students who've died suddenly, without a warning symptom or in freakish accidents. I've also seen friends live on for more than a decade after doctors had given them months or weeks to live.

We cannot predict the moment of our passing. Yet we know it will be among the most important days of our lives. In fact, all of Christian life can be seen as preparation for death.

Nevertheless, it's good for us to make distinctions between *remote* preparation and *near* preparation, because there are some things we should do differently if we know death is imminent, whether the death is our own, or a friend's or family member's.

The best preparation—and best done as far in advance as possible—is to make a good and thorough confession while we're still thinking clearly and still have energy for the task. Nothing brings peace to a soul like a confession that's well prepared: clear, concise, contrite, and complete. If we haven't been to confession in a while—and even if we have—we should make every effort to make the practice *habitual* during our final illness.

We should make arrangements to receive sacramental anointing, as soon as we know we're gravely ill (see chapter 22). We should also make arrangements to receive Holy Communion as often as possible, either by attending Mass or by alerting the hospital chaplain or local parish. It's important that we make the contact. Because of privacy laws, medical personnel are usually prevented from contacting clergy unless a patient explicitly asks. In the olden days, Catholics were known to wear a medal or carry a card that read: "I am a Catholic. In case of emergency, please call a priest." I've seen Catholic-school identification cards that had the line printed in boldface, all capital letters, just below the student's photograph. I don't know if such an item would provide the requisite legal license for anyone to make the call, but it just might prompt a doctor or nurse to ask our permission. In any event, it's a powerful witness to the importance of the faith, and it may be the last act that's reckoned to us as righteousness. When my friend's father insisted on wearing a scapular during his hospital stay—and explained why—he inspired all the attending medical personnel to ask for scapulars, too!

As we are dying, it's important for us to be clear about our business, and to keep it before us. We are working toward a goal, and we want to accomplish it in good time. If we spend all our time trying to distract ourselves from the thought, we'll fail eventually, because the thought is overwhelming, and we'll make more misery for ourselves at the end, because we'll be unprepared.

So it's good for us to follow after the saints and think hard about the "four last things": death, judgment, heaven, and hell. The Church encourages us to do this even while we're healthy, so that we're always viewing our days from an eternal perspective. Surely you've seen paintings of the cells of monks who kept a human skull on their work tables. We need not go to such lengths as acquiring a skull for our bed stand, but traveling usually goes more smoothly and swiftly when we have a clear idea of our destination. In our prayer, in the presence of God, we should think about death.

Nor should this make us somber or dreary. Those monks kept a good sense of humor even as they faced the inevitable. St. Thomas More—a layman, a lawyer, and father to a large family—was even able to joke with his executioner as he ascended the scaffold. It's not unseemly for a Christian to have a laugh at death's expense. And whether we're the caregiver or the care receiver, we should never underestimate the value of our smile. I know of a dying man who "practiced" his smile for an hour before his visiting nurse arrived every day. "Those people have to see so much suffering all day long," he explained. "I want to make their way a little easier." Now that's heroic Christian charity, and I'm sure it cost him dearly, but he never had to spend a cent, and I'm sure it left him feeling better, too. We should remind ourselves often that a death sentence is a normal part of life and not a license to make others miserable through our carelessness. We should care as much as we can, and care to keep our humor.

The Catholic novelist Muriel Spark often had to defend herself against critics who said she was cruel for joking about death. She responded to them: "I'm often very deadpan, but there's a moral statement too, and what it's saying is that there's a life beyond this, and these events are not the most important things."

Yet they are important, because they're the stuff of the life that remains to us, and so we take care with them. If it's our own death we're preparing for, we should try to get our affairs in order, so that those who survive us won't have quite so much work to do. We can look upon this as our professional work during the last leg of the journey. We can, then, offer it as prayer, as we would offer any of our ordinary labors. It's a good task that will keep us occupied, if not distracted, and at the same time keep us moving toward our goal. Like much human work, it can be a genuine act of love. We should not, however, put undue pressure on ourselves to finish the job. One does what one can.

It's good for us to have instructions in place, so that those who care for us know our wishes. This is especially true if we're cared for by people who don't share our faith. We can help them to understand our preferences for medical treatment. We can catechize them on the differences between "ordinary" and "extraordinary" means. We can help them to know that it's never licit to cause death intentionally, even if a patient is suffering. We can witness to the value of suffering voluntarily borne.

We can even do more than that. We can "offer it up." Bishop Fulton Sheen said that, whenever he passed a hospital, he was saddened to think of how much suffering goes "wasted," when it could be put to use. We can indeed unite our sufferings with those of Jesus Christ (see Col 1:24) and thus rescue them from meaninglessness. We can make them redemptive. Our pains and discomforts, our fears and humiliations can redeem with the power of Christ. Bishop Sheen urged caregivers and medical professionals to let their suffering friends in on this "secret." So should we.

Nor is the Catholic faith indifferent to the destination of our bodies after death. The Church prefers that we choose a Catholic cemetery for the burial of our mortal remains, as a sign of our belief in the resurrection of the body. Our flesh has been divinized in baptism, made one with the flesh of Jesus in Holy Communion, and so its repose is a matter of some consequence. That's why

Christians have always treated their cemeteries as holy ground, sacred space.

This is not a strict obligation. However, if we choose another burial site, we should make arrangements for a priest or deacon to bless the crypt. The Church's law now permits the cremation of the remains of the faithful, but again we should make proper arrangements so that the committal and repose take place according to the rites of the Church.

When death at last is imminent, we should call upon the Church to provide Viaticum, the last sacraments. (The Latin word suggests wayfarers' food, bread for the journey.) The rites are beautiful and genuinely helpful for keeping the dying person focused on the task. They provide an opportunity for a last expression of sorrow for sins and a last profession of the Catholic faith. When we are caregivers, we too can help by reading from a spiritual book during those last days, or simply praying prayers of aspiration aloud, something suitable for the dying person to repeat or think about. If it's our own death we're preparing for, we might consider making such reading materials available to our caregivers, along with instructions. Again, we shouldn't minimize the evangelistic and catechetical value of our dying days. They are a sign and a mystery to those who survive. One person's death is very often the occasion of another's conversion.

When we face death as Christians, we're like babies waiting to be born. Our faces press up against a membrane that separates us from a life we cannot see and could not possibly understand. The words of the Mass of Christian Burial bear repeating: "life is changed, not ended." Cardinal Newman said it in words that were a great comfort to me at the time of my father's death. They remain a great comfort to me even today, after so many years and so many more partings: "all who ever lived still live."

You and I, too, shall pass. And yet, dying, behold we live (see 2 Cor 6:9).

Ponder in Your Heart

Nothing is more difficult than to realize that every man has a distinct soul, that every one of all the millions who live or have lived, is as whole and independent a being in himself, as if there were no one else in the whole world but he . . . Every one of those souls still lives. They had their separate thoughts and feelings when on earth, they have them now. They had their likings and pursuits; they gained what they thought good and enjoyed it; and they still somewhere or other live, and what they then did in the flesh surely has its influence upon their present destiny. They live, reserved for a day which is to come, when all nations shall stand before God.

—John Henry Cardinal Newman, nineteenth century

40.

Prayers for the Dead

Some years ago I made a pilgrimage to Rome with a dear friend. I didn't know it at the time, but one of his intentions for the journey was a healing. He wanted Our Lord to "fix" the conflicted emotions he felt toward his father, who had been dead for many years. My friend was indeed healed, at one of the holy sites, by a sudden rush of grace, manifest in an overflow of tears.

Dazzled and bewildered, he went to our pilgrim chaplain, Father Joseph Linck, for wisdom to understand what had just happened. An experienced spiritual director, Father Joe explained the moment in terms of the Communion of Saints—all the connections between the living and the dead. He concluded with words I hope never to forget: "Relationships don't end."

My friend knew, from that moment, that he had a duty to pray for his father's soul. He knew, too, that he should not hesitate to ask prayers of his father. He was, in short, reconciling with his father and picking up their relationship where it should have left off.

God, in his mercy, has made this possible for us. Life is short, and we don't always have the time or wisdom to love people as we should, as they deserve to be loved. Sometimes we don't even recognize the debt we owe others until long after they're gone, and it's too late to thank them. If relationships ended with death, then this would be an immense tragedy: an utterly lost opportunity, a perpetually raw wound.

The doctrine of purgatory actually dates back to the Old Testament. The Second Book of Maccabees (12:39–46) tells of when Judas Maccabeus found pagan amulets on the bodies of dead Jewish soldiers—a sign that they had sinned by practicing idolatry. Judas "then took up a collection among all his soldiers . . . which he sent to Jerusalem to provide for an expiatory sacrifice . . . Thus he made atonement for the dead that they might be freed from this sin." The passage concludes: "It is a holy and wholesome thought to pray for the dead."

In Judaism, similar practices were common at the time of Jesus' earthly ministry. They endure today in the prayers known as the "mourner's kaddish," offered after a family member's death, and *El Male Rachamim*, which specifically concerns the soul of the deceased.

The New Testament continues to speak of purgatory, though only implicitly. In Matthew's Gospel, Jesus says that "whoever speaks against the Holy Spirit will not be forgiven, either in this age or in the age to come" (Mt 12:32). Thus, he implies that there is some way of forgiveness in the age to come. St. Paul taught that Christians who are less than completely faithful "will be saved, but only as it were through fire" (1 Cor 3:15). That metaphorical "fire" is the purification of purgatory.

The book of Revelation (21:27) says, "nothing unclean will enter" heaven. Purgatory is simply the stage after death when the soul is purified of all uncleanness—the effects of a lifetime's sins. It seems that most, if not all, of those who get to heaven must pass through this stage. As St. Paul said, "All have sinned and fall short of the glory of God" (Rom 3:23).

If we confess our sins, God forgives us. Yet we still need to be healed of the damage we've done to ourselves. This healing, like earthly healing, may involve suffering. Medicine sometimes tastes bad and even makes us feel queasy. Physical therapy can leave us sore. But the doctor does not prescribe those remedies because of their unwanted side effects; he prescribes them because they heal. Sometimes healing hurts. The Catholic novelist Flannery O'Connor applied this principle to the doctrine of purgatory: "Water is a symbol of purification and fire is another. Water, it seems to me, is a symbol of the kind of purification that God gives irrespective of our efforts or worthiness, and fire is the kind of purification we bring on ourselves—as in Purgatory. It is our evil which is naturally burnt away when it comes anywhere near God."

This is certainly how the early Christians read the Gospels. The catacombs and other ancient Christian burial places bear witness to early concern for the souls of the dead. Christian families often carved onto gravestones pleas for passersby to remember the departed. In the late second century, the North African Christian Tertullian spoke of purgatory, as did his countryman St. Cyprian in the third century. At the same time, we find the doctrine in the writings of Origen in Egypt. St. Augustine's mother, St. Monica, urged him to offer Mass for her after she died. And St. John Chrysostom urged his congregation to have the liturgy offered for the dead: "Let us help and commemorate them. If Job's sons were purified by their father's sacrifice [see Jb 1:5], why would we doubt that our offerings for the dead bring them some consolation? Let us not hesitate to help those who have died and to offer our prayers for them."

This is the faith of the Church of Jesus Christ, and it has always been so. From the Old Testament through the New, from the Apostolic Fathers through the medieval scholastics, no one dared to question the continuity of relationships among Christians. Those who remained on earth had a way of relating to those who had gone on in death. Only with the Protestant Reformation was this taken away. The Lutheran theologian Frank Senn put the matter succinctly: Martin Luther's "abolition of votive Masses, especially those offered for the dead, contributed to undermining the more cosmic understanding of the Church . . ."

But the Catholic Church could neither abolish nor undermine the Christian tradition. Doctrine can be neither created nor destroyed, neither altered nor ended. So we still pray in the Mass of Christian Burial: "Lord, for your faithful people life is changed, not ended." Or, as Father Joe said more colloquially to my friend in Rome: "Relationships don't end." We may pray for the dead, and thank God for that. He is merciful, and his mercy endures *forever!*

Ponder in Your Heart

David also says: "For his steadfast love endures forever!" By which saying it is plain, that in whatever state a man leaves this life, in the same state he is presented in judgment before God.

Yet we must believe that before the day of judgment there is a purgatory fire for certain small sins: because our Saviour says, that whoever speaks blasphemy against the Holy Spirit, it shall not be forgiven him, neither in this world, nor in the world to come. From which sentence we learn that some sins are forgiven in this world, and some others may be pardoned in the next: for what is denied concerning one sin, is therefore understood to be granted concerning some other.

Still, as I said, we have to believe this only about little and very small sins—such as, for example, daily idle talk, immoderate laughter . . . (hardly anyone can avoid these offenses) . . . and ignorant errors in matters of no great weight. All these sins will be punished after death, if we did not obtain pardon and remission for them in our lifetime.

For St. Paul says that Christ is the foundation, and in a while adds: "And if any man build upon this foundation gold, silver, precious stones, wood, hay, stubble: the work of every one, of what kind it is, the fire shall try." If what you build on that foundation abides, you shall receive reward; if it burns, you shall suffer loss, but you yourself shall be saved, though as if by fire.

We might take these words to mean the fire of tribulation that we suffer in this world. But if you would interpret them as meaning the fire of purgatory in the next life, then you must carefully consider that the Apostle did not say that you may be saved by fire if you build on this foundation iron, brass, or lead—that is, the greater sort of sins, and therefore more hard, and consequently not remissible in that place. But you will be saved by fire if you build wood, hay, stubble—that is, little and very light sins, which the fire easily burns up. Yet we have here further to consider, that none can be there purged—no, not for the tiniest sins—unless in his lifetime he deserved by virtuous works to find such favor in that place.

—Pope St. Gregory the Great, sixth century

Epilogue

Jesus said to his disciples: "Ask, and it will be given you; seek, and you will find; knock, and it will be opened to you" (Mt 7:7).

Ask, seek, knock. We may be sure that he was not merely running down a list of quaint metaphors for prayer. More likely he was describing what everyone would recognize as the itinerary for a pilgrimage to the holy city. Pilgrims begin by asking the way. They travel in search of their destination: they seek. And they arrive as they knock at the city gates.

The way of Christian prayer is the way of a pilgrim. It is in the Sermon on the Mount that Jesus makes this connection. Jesus gives his teaching on pilgrimage immediately after he spells out his guidelines for the disciplines of prayer, fasting, and almsgiving (see Mt 6). From these words, all Catholic devotion has come forth, in all its richness and diversity. We have not yet begun to exhaust the possibilities for expressing our love, praise, thanksgiving, longing, wonder, and contrition.

Jesus left us with something to do. He left us not simply with a ready-made, gift-wrapped salvation, with all our questions answered and all our suffering ceased. Instead, he bid us to follow him along a road—a narrow road, to a narrow gate—in a great adventure. His road leads us to glory, but only by way of Calvary. We don't really know what awaits us around the next bend in the road; but we know that God is with us and he will answer us when we ask, seek, and knock—as we pray in the old accustomed ways.

All our lives, we are on pilgrimage. I began this book with the story of my late-night journey to the cross, my late-night Rosary on my neighborhood streets. I've come to learn, however, that my identity as a wayfarer is not occasional, but semi-permanent. For no longer do we journey to an earthly city, as Jesus' disciples did in the first century. Our Jerusalem is above, and we'll be asking, seeking, knocking till we're there. No longer do we seek an earthly temple; for God is building us up, by means of our prayer, as a heavenly temple.

So this book ends as it began. Beloved, we are God's children now, but we're not home yet. God is our Father, but he's in heaven. That's why we face crises, to remind us that we're pilgrims, still on the way. The Father uses these moments to change us, to speed us along the way, to transform pilgrims into saints.

We ask, seek, knock. We go our pilgrim way. We find the grace we need—though not always the grace we'd wish for, or the grace we'd expect. We receive the grace a perfect Father would give to his children who are on their way home.

Notes

Introduction

11. **Pope St. Leo the Great said:** St. Leo the Great, Sermon 74.2; see also *Catechism of the Catholic Church* (hereafter CCC), n. 1115.
11. **Pope Benedict XVI once said:** *Sacramentum Caritas* 64.
12. **"There are many things":** St. Gregory of Nyssa, *On the Baptism of Christ,* in Scott Hahn and Mike Aquilina, *Living the Mysteries* (Huntington, IN: Our Sunday Visitor, 2003), 44.

Chapter 1: Holy Water

21. **At the end of the second century:** Tertullian, *On Prayer* 13.
22. **St. Thomas Aquinas taught:** For a fuller discussion of St. Thomas's method, see my essay "Search the Scriptures: Reading the Old Testament with Jesus, John and Thomas Aquinas," in *Scripture Matters: Essays on Reading the Bible from the Heart of the Church* (Steubenville, OH: Emmaus Road, 2003).
22. **With Jesus, however:** St. Thomas Aquinas, *Commentary on St. John* 443.

23. **According to St. Thomas:** Ibid., 577.
23. **St. Teresa of Avila wrote:** St. Teresa of Avila, *The Book of Her Life* 31.4, in *Saint Teresa of Avila: Collected Works,* trans. Kieran Kavanaugh, vol. 1, (Washington, D.C.: ICS, 1987), 265.
24. **King and Lord of all things:** Adapted from the Wobbermin translation, *Bishop Sarapion's Prayer-Book* (London: SPCK, 1899), 68–69.

Chapter 2: The Sign of the Cross

25. **Cardinal Joseph Ratzinger (the future Pope Benedict XVI):** Joseph Cardinal Ratzinger, *The Spirit of the Liturgy* (San Francisco: Ignatius, 2000), 177.
26. **At the end of the second century:** Tertullian, *The Chaplet* 3.
26. **Tertullian praised his wife:** Tertullian, *To His Wife* 2.5.
27. **We raise the hand first:** St. Francis de Sales, *The Standard of the Cross* 3.1, quoted in Nicholas Gihr, *The Holy Sacrifice of the Mass* (St. Louis: Herder, 1939), 349-350. Language modernized slightly.
27. **The cross is an image:** For a fuller treatment of the relationship between the Trinity and the cross, see my book *First Comes Love: Finding Your Family in the Church and the Trinity,* 2nd ed. (New York: Doubleday, 2002).
28. **In his groundbreaking work:** St. Basil the Great, *On the Holy Spirit* 27.66.
29. **It is, in the words of Cardinal Ratzinger:** Ratzinger, *The Spirit of the Liturgy,* 178.
29. **"Making the sign of the Cross":** Pope Benedict XVI, Angelus address, September 11, 2005.
29. **When we cross ourselves:** Romano Guardini, *Sacred Signs* (St. Louis: Pio Decimo, 1956), 13–14.

Chapter 3: Baptism

30. **Life begins at baptism:** For a fuller treatment of baptism, see my book *Swear to God: The Promise and Power of the Sacraments* (New York: Doubleday, 2004).
33. **Yet baptism, he said:** St. Ambrose of Milan, Letter 72 (to Constantius), par. 16.
34. **"We are Christians because of a covenant":** Romano Guardini, *Meditations Before Mass* (Manchester, NH: Sophia Institute Press, 1993), 191.
35. **In considering . . . the gift:** Pope John Paul II, apostolic exhortation *Christifideles Laici* (On the Vocation and Mission of the Lay Faithful in the Church and in the World), nn. 11 and 17, December 30, 1988.

Chapter 4: The Mass

37. **Long before the New Testament books:** I have explored the Mass in many books, among them *The Lamb's Supper: The Mass as Heaven on Earth* (New York: Doubleday, 1999); *Swear to God: The Promise and Power of the Sacraments* (New York: Doubleday, 2004); *Letter and Spirit: From Written Text to Living Word in the Liturgy* (New York: Doubleday, 2005); and *Catholic for a Reason III: Scripture and the Mystery of the Mass* (Steubenville, OH: Emmaus Road, 2004).
38. **Many years before he became pope:** See his discussion in *Behold the Pierced One* (San Francisco: Ignatius, 1986), 83–85.
41. **Here we must apply our minds:** St. John Chrysostom, Homily 14 on Hebrews, n. 3.

Chapter 5: Guardian Angels

47. **Let us look for a moment:** St. Josemaría Escrivá, *Christ Is Passing By* (Princeton, NJ: Scepter, no date), 139–141.

Chapter 6: The Church's Calendar

51. **The catechism of the Jew:** Samson Raphael Hirsch, *Judaism Eternal* (London: Soncino, no date), 3.

55. **People are instructed in the truths:** Pope Pius XI, encyclical letter *Quas Primas* (On the Feast of Christ the King), nn. 21–22, December 11, 1925.

Chapter 7: Lent and Easter

59. **Lent is the season:** St. John Cassian, *Conferences* 21.28.

60. **In the words of St. Athanasius:** St. Athanasius, *Festal Letter* 3.5.

61. **A second-century bishop put it this way:** St. Melito of Sardis, Paschal Homily 20.7.

61. **We firmly believe:** St. Augustine, quoted in Thomas Spidlík, ed., *Drinking from the Hidden Fountain: A Patristic Breviary* (Kalamazoo, MI: Cistercian Publications, 1994), 338.

Chapter 8: Advent and Christmas

67. **Advent is celebrated for four weeks:** Jacobus de Voragine, *The Golden Legend* (London: Longmans, Green, 1941), 2-3 (language modernized slightly).

Chapter 9: Novenas

70. **But the Church recommends:** See n. 189 in the *Directory on Popular Piety and the Liturgy: Principles and Guidelines,* published by the Vatican's Congregation for Divine Worship in 2001.

70. **Pope Benedict XVI has wished:** Pope Benedict XVI, *Address to the Members of the Italian Armed Forces,* December 16, 2005.

71. **Blessed Pope John XXIII:** See his encyclical letter *Paenitentiam Agere,* n. 26.

73. **The Acts of the Apostles reminds us:** Pope John Paul II, homily in Beirut, Lebanon, May 11, 1997.

Chapter 10: Posture

77. **We are composed of body and soul:** Guardini, *Sacred Signs,* 15.
78. **In the second case, as Cardinal Ratzinger said poetically:** Joseph Cardinal Ratzinger, *The Spirit of the Liturgy* (San Francisco: Ignatius Press, 2000), 188.
79. **Here's Father Guardini again:** Guardini, *Sacred Signs* (St. Louis, MO: Pio Decimo, 1955), 22.
80. **Pope John Paul II was able to build:** Pope John Paul II, general audience, December 19, 1979.
80. **The physical postures assumed:** Congregation for Divine Worship, *The Year of the Eucharist: Suggestions and Proposals,* October 15, 2004.

Chapter 11: Morning Offering

86. **In 2005 the Synod of Bishops:** Vatican summary of intervention by Archbishop Luciano Pedro Mendes de Almeida, SJ, of Mariana, Brazil, at the Synod of Bishops, October 6, 2005.
87. **The supreme and eternal Priest:** Vatican Council II, *The Dogmatic Constitution on the Church: Lumen Gentium,* n. 34 (November 21, 1964).

Chapter 12: Prayers of Aspiration

90. **St. Augustine put it well:** St. Augustine, *Letters* 130.10.19-20.
93. **Aspire continually to God:** St. Francis de Sales, *Introduction to the Devout Life,* 2.13. Adapted from the translation of John K. Ryan (New York: Doubleday, 2003), 88.

Chapter 13: The Angelus

96. **All subsequent history:** I treat these and other Marian themes at greater length in my books *Hail, Holy Queen: The Mother of God in the Word of God* (New York: Doubleday, 2001) and *Catholic for a Reason II: Scripture and the Mystery of the Mother of God,* 2nd ed. (Steubenville, OH: Emmaus Road, 2004).

97. **The early Christians remembered:** Tertullian, *On Prayer* 25.
98. **What we have to say:** Pope Paul VI, apostolic exhortation *Marialis Cultis,* n. 41, February 2, 1974.

Chapter 14: Grace at Meals

101. **The invocation of the Lord:** Baruch Levine, *Leviticus* (Philadelphia: Jewish Publication Society, 1989), xxxviii.
103. **O Lord our God:** Quoted in A. Hamman, ed., *Early Christian Prayers* (Chicago: Regnery, 1961), 147.

Chapter 15: Examination of Conscience

108. **In the morning, as soon as you wake:** Pope John XXIII, "Little Rules of Ascetic Life," in *Journal of a Soul* (New York: Signet, 1965), 479–480.

Chapter 16: Bible Study

111. **We live in a time:** I have written many books on the study of Scripture. See, for example, *Scripture Matters* and *Letter and Spirit.* I am co-editor of the *Ignatius Catholic Study Bible* (San Francisco: Ignatius Press). See also the free online Bible studies at salvationhistory.com.
116. **I remember our Latvian priest:** Bishop Antons Justs of Jelgava, Latvia, quoted in the proceedings from the 2008 Synod on the Word of God in the Life and Mission of the Church.

Chapter 17: Spiritual Reading

118. **One of the leading lights:** St. Epiphanius of Cyprus, quoted in Benedicta Ward, *The Sayings of the Desert Fathers* (Kalamazoo, MI: Cistercian Publications: 1984), 58.
119. **A Carthusian abbot named Guigo II:** You'll find Guigo quoted in the CCC, n. 2654. But his great work, *The Ladder from Earth to Heaven,* is itself excellent material for spiritual reading. It's available in a very

readable new translation in *The Authority of Mystery: The Word of God and the People of God,* volume 2 of *Letter and Spirit: A Journal of Biblical Theology* (Steubenville, OH: Emmaus Road, 2006), 175ff.

119. **Indeed, I know a few such men:** Both Father John Hardon, SJ, and Father C. John McCloskey have published lists with the title "Catholic Lifetime Reading Plan." Father McCloskey's is available free online. Father Hardon's is available from Grotto Press.

120. **One of my favorite spiritual writers, Eugene Boylan:** M. Eugene Boylan, *This Tremendous Lover* (Westminster, MD: Christian Classics, 1989), 123.

120. **Father Boylan also emphasized:** Ibid., 119, 116.

121. **Father Boylan said:** Ibid., 113.

122. **I send you the book on Christian hope:** J.-P. de Caussade, *Abandonment to Divine Providence* (St. Louis: Herder, 1921), 201.

Chapter 18. Retreat

128. **I made this retreat:** Dorothy Day, quoted in Brigid O'Shea Merriman, *Searching for Christ: The Spirituality of Dorothy Day* (Notre Dame, IN: University of Notre Dame Press, 1994), 165.

Chapter 19: Confirmation

131. **To be saved means nothing less:** I discuss Confirmation, with the other sacraments, in my book *Swear to God.*

133. **The Church teaches that confirmation:** See CCC, n. 1304.

134. **Now that you have been "baptized into Christ":** St. Cyril of Jerusalem, *Mystagogical Sermons* 3.1–3, in Edward Yarnold, *The Awe-Inspiring Rites of Initiation* (Collegeville, MN: Liturgical Press, 1994), 81–83.

Chapter 20: Marriage

136. **In John's apocalypse:** I discuss marriage at greater length in my books *Swear to God, First Comes Love,* and *Catholic for a Reason IV: Scripture and the Mystery of Marriage and Family Life* (Steubenville, OH: Emmaus Road, 2007).

137. **Jon Levenson, a contemporary Jewish scholar:** Jon Levenson, *Sinai and Zion: An Entry into the Jewish Bible* (San Francisco: HarperCollins, 1985), 76.

137. **He goes on to explain:** Ibid., 77.

137. **Levenson concludes:** Ibid., 79.

137. **Rabbi Michael Fishbane traces:** Michael Fishbane, *JPS Bible Commentary: Haftarot* (Philadelphia: Jewish Publication Society, 2002), 555–556.

141. **"Every celebration," Augustine said:** Quoted in Claude Chavasse, *The Bride of Christ* (London: Faber and Faber, 1939), 147.

142. **Marriage has God for its Author:** Pope Leo XIII, encyclical letter *Arcanum Divinae,* n. 19, February 10, 1880.

Chapter 21: Priesthood

143. **After years of researching and praying:** I discuss Holy Orders in my books *Swear to God* and *Scripture Matters.*

147. **St. Augustine looked the same way:** St. Augustine, *Reflections on the Psalms* 44.32, quoted in Henri de Lubac, *The Motherhood of the Church* (San Francisco: Ignatius Press, 1982), 90.

148. **The reason that God-loving men of old:** Eusebius of Caesarea, *Demonstration of the Gospel* 1.9, quoted in Stefan Heid, *Celibacy in the Early Church* (San Francisco: Ignatius Press, 2000), 119.

Chapter 22: Anointing of the Sick

150. **This is the sacrament we know:** I discuss this, with the other sacraments, at greater length in my book *Swear to God.*

152. **The Old and the New Testament:** Aimé Georges Martimort, *The Signs of the New Covenant* (Collegeville, MN: Liturgical Press, 1963), 264–265, 268.

Chapter 23: Incense

159. **A Jewish theologian of the first century:** Philo of Alexandria, *The Special Laws* 1.171.
160. **Sovereign Lord Jesus Christ:** *Liturgy of St. James,* adapted from vol. 7 of *Ante-Nicene Fathers* (1994; repr., Peabody, MA: Hendrickson, 2004), 537, 540, 549.

Chapter 24: Candles

162. **In his commentary on Leviticus:** Levine, *Leviticus,* 217.
164. **The greatest Scripture scholar:** St. Jerome, *Against Vigilantius* 7.
164. **Jerome recalls the funeral:** St. Jerome, *Letters* 108.
164. **numberous wicks:** St. Jerome, *Against Vigilantius* 7.
164. **St. Paulinus of Nola described:** St. Paulinus of Nola, *Carmen* 111.
165. **The lamps that you kindle:** St. Gregory Nazianzen, *Oration* 40.46.

Chapter 25: Sacred Images

168. **The most eloquent of the iconodules:** St. Theodore of Studion, quoted in Christoph Schonborn, *God's Human Face* (San Francisco: Ignatius, 1994), 234.
169. **Since some find fault:** St. John of Damascus, *Exposition of the Orthodox Faith* 4.16.

Chapter 26: Relics

174. **The emperor Julian:** Julian the Apostate, quoted in Peter Brown, *The Cult of the Saints: Its Rise and Function in Latin Christianity* (Chicago: University of Chicago Press, 1982), 7.
175. **Addressed to a heretic:** St. Jerome, *Against Vigilantius* 5.

Chapter 27: Fasting and Mortification

180. **Let us fall to fasting:** St. Thomas More, quoted in E. E. Reynolds, ed., *The Heart of Thomas More* (London: Burns and Oates, 1966), 170–171.

Chapter 28: Confession

185. **Confession is the way:** My book-length study of confession is *Lord, Have Mercy: The Healing Power of Confession* (New York: Doubleday, 2003).
189. **the teaching we find in the *Didache*:** *Didache* 4.14.
189. **A later chapter speaks:** Ibid. 14.1.
190. **It is better to confess:** St. Clement of Rome, *To the Corinthians* 51.

Chapter 29: Indulgences

194. **There reigns among men:** Pope Paul VI, apostolic constitution *Indulgentiarum Doctrina*, chap. 2, January 1, 1967.

Chapter 30: Intercession of the Saints

199. **St. John Chrysostom, in the fourth century:** St. John Chrysostom, "On All the Martyrs," in *The Cult of the Saints* (Crestwood, NY: St. Vladimir Seminary Press, 2006), 247.
200. **St. Augustine preached often:** St. Augustine, *Sermons* 325.1.
200. **The fourth-century bishop St. Paulinus:** St. Paulinus of Nola, *Carmina* 21.
201. **To such figures we do not hesitate:** I discuss the Communion of Saints at greater length in my book *Reasons to Believe: How to Understand, Explain, and Defend the Catholic Faith* (New York: Doubleday, 2007).
201. **It is true that Christians:** St. Augustine, *Reply to Faustus* 20.21; see also *City of God* 8.27.

Chapter 31: Pilgrimage

205. **St. Augustine portrays believers:** St. Augustine, *City of God* 19.17.
206. **Pope John Paul II evoked the pilgrim road:** Pope John Paul II, address during the Rite of the Pilgrim, Cathedral of Santiago de Compostela, August 19, 1989.
207. **Paula entered Jerusalem:** St. Jerome, *Letters* 108.9.

Chapter 32: The Presence of God

212. **In the beginning of his novitiate:** Brother Lawrence, *Practice of the Presence of God,* Conversation 4 (adapted slightly).

Chapter 33: Almsgiving

215. **Consider the words of St. John Chrysostom:** St. John Chrysostom, *Homilies on Matthew* 50.3–4, quoted in Pope John Paul II, encyclical letter *Ecclesia de Eucharistia,* n. 34, April 17, 2003.
215. **around the year A.D. 107:** St. Ignatius of Antioch, *Letter to the Smyrnaeans* 7.
216. **Robert Ellsberg said of her:** Robert Ellsberg, lecture given at the New York University Symposium honoring Dorothy Day's centenary, November 8, 1997. Archived online at CatholicWorker.org.
216. **The Anglican scholar Gregory Dix:** Gregory Dix, *The Shape of the Liturgy* (New York: Seabury, 1982).
217. **the sociologist Robert Bellah:** Robert N. Bellah, "Religion and the Shape of National Culture," *America,* July 31/August 7, 1999, pp. 9–14.
218. **Christ understood that we have:** Blessed Mother Teresa of Calcutta, quoted in David Scott, *A Revolution of Love: The Meaning of Mother Teresa* (Chicago: Loyola Press, 2005), 88.

Chapter 34: Devotion to the Trinity

221. **We Christians tend:** My book *First Comes Love* is an extended discussion of the Trinity.

224. **Pope John Paul II proposed that:** Pope John Paul II, *Letter to Families,* n. 6, February 2, 1994 (italics in original).

225. **The same pope put the matter:** Pope John Paul II, *Puebla: A Pilgrimage of Faith* (Boston: Daughters of St. Paul, 1979), 86.

225. **To us ignorant people it appears:** St. Teresa of Avila, quoted in Kieran Kavanaugh, ed., *Teresa of Avila: The Way of Prayer* (Hyde Park, NY: New City Press, 2003), 102.

Chapter 35: The Rosary

227. **We call the Virgin Mary "blessed":** For a fuller discussion of the Church's Marian doctrine and piety, see my books *Hail, Holy Queen* and *Catholic for a Reason II.*

230. **In the years just before his election:** Joseph Cardinal Ratzinger, *God and the World* (San Francisco: Ignatius, 2002), 319.

230. **Mother Teresa of Calcutta endured a harrowing vision:** Mother Teresa, *Come Be My Light* (New York: Doubleday, 2007), 99.

232. **The Rosary, though clearly Marian:** Pope John Paul II, apostolic letter *Rosarium Mariae Virginis,* n. 1, October 16, 2002 (italics in original).

Chapter 36: Scapulars and Medals

234. **The word *scapular* comes from:** For the earliest history of the scapular, see Elizabeth Kuhns, *The Habit: A History of the Clothing of Catholic Nuns* (New York: Doubleday, 2003), 67–69.

236. **St. Thérèse of Lisieux said:** St. Thérèse of Lisieux, letter to her sister Celine, in *Letters of St. Thérèse of Lisieux,* vol. 2 (Washington: ICS Publications, 1982), 866.

236. **The sign of the Scapular points:** Pope John Paul II, *Message to the Carmelite Family,* n. 5, March 25, 2001.

Chapter 37: Mental Prayer

238. **St. Teresa of Avila summed it up:** St. Teresa of Avila, *The Book of Her Life* 8.5, in *The Collected Works of St. Teresa of Avila,* transl. and ed. Kieran Kavanaugh and Otilio Rodriguez, vol. 1 (Washington, DC: Institute for Carmelite Studies, 1976), 67.

241. **Mental prayer consists of:** St. Teresa of Avila, *The Way of Perfection* 25.3, in *The Collected Works of St. Teresa of Avila,* transl. and ed. Kieran Kavanaugh and Otilio Rodriguez, vol. 2 (Washington, DC: Institute for Carmelite Studies, 1980), 131–132.

Chapter 38: Reverence for the Tabernacle

243. **According to Church law:** *Code of Canon Law,* canon 938.

244. **We learn altar piety:** *Didascalia Apostolorum* 9, in Lucien Deiss, *Springtime of the Liturgy* (Collegeville, MN: Liturgical Press, 1979), 174.

244. **My mother used to take me for walks:** Ronald Lawler, "Ordinary Faith in the Eucharist," *Catholic Dossier,* September/October 1996, 28–30.

Chapter 39: Preparation for Death

251. **The Catholic novelist Muriel Spark:** Muriel Spark, quoted in Helen T. Vorongos and Alan Cowell, "Muriel Spark, Novelist Who Wrote 'The Prime of Miss Jean Brodie,' Dies at 88," *New York Times,* April 16, 2006.

254. **Nothing is more difficult:** John Henry Cardinal Newman, "The Individuality of the Soul," in *Parochial and Plain Sermons,* vol. 4 (London: Longmans, Green, 1909), 80–81, 83–84.

Chapter 40: Prayers for the Dead

256. **The doctrine of purgatory:** For a fuller discussion of the doctrine, see my book *Reasons to Believe.*

257. **The Catholic novelist Flannery O'Connor:** Flannery O'Connor, *The Habit of Being* (New York: Vintage, 1980), 387.

257. **St. John Chrysostom urged his congregations:** St. John Chrysostom, *Homilies on First Corinthians* 41.5.

258. **The Lutheran theologian Frank Senn:** Frank C. Senn, "Sacraments and Social History: Postmodern Practice," *Theology Today,* October 2001, 294.

258. **David also says:** Pope St. Gregory the Great, *Dialogues* 4.39.